## Telecommunications Analysis
## Complete Self-Assessment Guid

C000140971

The guidance in this Self-Assessment is b
Analysis best practices and standards in business process architecture,
design and quality management. The guidance is also based on the
professional judgment of the individual collaborators listed in the
Acknowledgments.

**Notice of rights**

**Trademarks**

# Table of Contents

# About The Art of Service

The Art of Service, Business Process Architects since 2000, is dedicated to helping stakeholders achieve excellence.

Defining, designing, creating, and implementing a process to solve a stakeholders challenge or meet an objective is the most valuable role… In EVERY group, company, organization and department.

Unless you're talking a one-time, single-use project, there should be a process. Whether that process is managed and implemented by humans, AI, or a combination of the two, it needs to be designed by someone with a complex enough perspective to ask the right questions.

Someone capable of asking the right questions and step back and say, 'What are we really trying to accomplish here? And is there a different way to look at it?'

With The Art of Service's Standard Requirements Self-Assessments, we empower people who can do just that — whether their title is marketer, entrepreneur, manager, salesperson, consultant, Business Process Manager, executive assistant, IT Manager, CIO etc... —they are the people who rule the future. They are people who watch the process as it happens, and ask the right questions to make the process work better.

**Contact us when you need any support with this Self-Assessment and any help with templates, blue-prints and examples of standard documents you might need:**

http://theartofservice.com
service@theartofservice.com

# Included Resources - how to access

Included with your purchase of the book is the

Telecommunications Analysis Self-Assessment Spreadsheet Dashboard which contains all questions and Self-Assessment areas and auto-generates insights, graphs, and project RACI planning - all with examples to get you started right away.

## How? Simply send an email to
**access@theartofservice.com**
with this books' title in the subject to get the Telecommunications Analysis Self Assessment Tool right away.

You will receive the following contents with New and Updated specific criteria:

- The latest quick edition of the book in PDF

- The latest complete edition of the book in PDF, which criteria correspond to the criteria in...

- The Self-Assessment Excel Dashboard, and...

- Example pre-filled Self-Assessment Excel Dashboard to get familiar with results generation

- In-depth specific Checklists covering the topic

- Project management checklists and templates to assist with implementation

# Purpose of this Self-Assessment

This Self-Assessment has been developed to improve understanding of the requirements and elements of Telecommunications Analysis, based on best practices and standards in business process architecture, design and quality management.

It is designed to allow for a rapid Self-Assessment to determine how closely existing management practices and procedures correspond to the elements of the Self-Assessment.

The criteria of requirements and elements of Telecommunications Analysis have been rephrased in the format of a Self-Assessment questionnaire, with a seven-criterion scoring system, as explained in this document.

In this format, even with limited background knowledge of Telecommunications Analysis, a manager can quickly review existing operations to determine how they measure up to the standards. This in turn can serve as the starting point of a 'gap analysis' to identify management tools or system elements that might usefully be implemented in the organization to help improve overall performance.

# How to use the Self-Assessment

On the following pages are a series of questions to identify to what extent your Telecommunications Analysis initiative is complete in comparison to the requirements set in standards.

To facilitate answering the questions, there is a space in front of each question to enter a score on a scale of '1' to '5'.

## 1 Strongly Disagree

## 2 Disagree

## 3 Neutral

## 4 Agree

## 5 Strongly Agree

*Read the question and rate it with the following in front of mind:*

## 'In my belief,
## the answer to this question is clearly defined'.

There are two ways in which you can choose to interpret this statement;
1. how aware are you that the answer to the question is clearly defined
2. for more in-depth analysis you can choose to gather evidence and confirm the answer to the question. This obviously will take more time, most Self-Assessment users opt for the first way to interpret the question and dig deeper later on based on the outcome of the

overall Self-Assessment.

A score of '1' would mean that the answer is not clear at all, where a '5' would mean the answer is crystal clear and defined. Leave emtpy when the question is not applicable or you don't want to answer it, you can skip it without affecting your score. Write your score in the space provided.

After you have responded to all the appropriate statements in each section, compute your average score for that section, using the formula provided, and round to the nearest tenth. Then transfer to the corresponding spoke in the Telecommunications Analysis Scorecard on the second next page of the Self-Assessment.

Your completed Telecommunications Analysis Scorecard will give you a clear presentation of which Telecommunications Analysis areas need attention.

# Telecommunications Analysis Scorecard Example

Example of how the finalized Scorecard can look like:

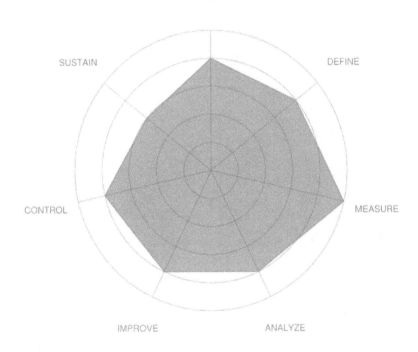

# Telecommunications Analysis Scorecard

Your Scores:

# BEGINNING OF THE SELF-ASSESSMENT:

# CRITERION #1: RECOGNIZE

INTENT: Be aware of the need for change. Recognize that there is an unfavorable variation, problem or symptom.

In my belief, the answer to this question is clearly defined:

5 Strongly Agree

4 Agree

3 Neutral

2 Disagree

1 Strongly Disagree

1. Whom do you really need or want to serve?
<--- Score

2. Are problem definition and motivation clearly presented?
<--- Score

**3. Are there Telecommunications Analysis problems defined?**

<--- Score

4. Is the quality assurance team identified?
<--- Score

5. How do you take a forward-looking perspective in identifying Telecommunications Analysis research related to market response and models?
<--- Score

6. Who else hopes to benefit from it?
<--- Score

7. What creative shifts do you need to take?
<--- Score

**8. What extra resources will you need?**
<--- Score

9. Did you miss any major Telecommunications Analysis issues?
<--- Score

**10. What is the Telecommunications Analysis problem definition? What do you need to resolve?**
<--- Score

11. Who needs to know about Telecommunications Analysis?
<--- Score

12. What is the recognized need?
<--- Score

13. Will new equipment/products be required to facilitate Telecommunications Analysis delivery, for

example is new software needed?

<--- Score

14. Have you identified your Telecommunications Analysis key performance indicators?

<--- Score

15. Are controls defined to recognize and contain problems?

<--- Score

**16. Does your organization need more Telecommunications Analysis education?**

<--- Score

**17. How are training requirements identified?**

<--- Score

18. What vendors make products that address the Telecommunications Analysis needs?

<--- Score

19. How are you going to measure success?

<--- Score

20. Is the need for organizational change recognized?

<--- Score

21. What information do users need?

<--- Score

22. Who should resolve the Telecommunications Analysis issues?

<--- Score

23. Looking at each person individually – does every

one have the qualities which are needed to work in this group?

<--- Score

24. When a Telecommunications Analysis manager recognizes a problem, what options are available?

<--- Score

25. Are there any specific expectations or concerns about the Telecommunications Analysis team, Telecommunications Analysis itself?

<--- Score

26. How do you recognize an Telecommunications Analysis objection?

<--- Score

27. What prevents you from making the changes you know will make you a more effective Telecommunications Analysis leader?

<--- Score

28. What does Telecommunications Analysis success mean to the stakeholders?

<--- Score

29. Who needs what information?

<--- Score

30. What needs to stay?

<--- Score

31. How do you identify the kinds of information that you will need?

<--- Score

32. To what extent does each concerned units management team recognize Telecommunications Analysis as an effective investment?
<--- Score

33. What is the problem or issue?
<--- Score

34. Where is training needed?
<--- Score

**35. Which issues are too important to ignore?**
<--- Score

36. Is it needed?
<--- Score

37. Can management personnel recognize the monetary benefit of Telecommunications Analysis?
<--- Score

**38. Will Telecommunications Analysis deliverables need to be tested and, if so, by whom?**
<--- Score

39. Are your goals realistic? Do you need to redefine your problem? Perhaps the problem has changed or maybe you have reached your goal and need to set a new one?
<--- Score

**40. What do you need to start doing?**
<--- Score

41. What are the clients issues and concerns?
<--- Score

42. Who defines the rules in relation to any given issue?
<--- Score

**43. Think about the people you identified for your Telecommunications Analysis project and the project responsibilities you would assign to them, what kind of training do you think they would need to perform these responsibilities effectively?**
<--- Score

**44. How does it fit into your organizational needs and tasks?**
<--- Score

45. What is the smallest subset of the problem you can usefully solve?
<--- Score

46. Who are your key stakeholders who need to sign off?
<--- Score

47. Will a response program recognize when a crisis occurs and provide some level of response?
<--- Score

48. Are there any revenue recognition issues?
<--- Score

49. What do employees need in the short term?
<--- Score

**50. What Telecommunications Analysis problem should be solved?**

<--- Score

**51. Where do you need to exercise leadership?**
<--- Score

52. Does Telecommunications Analysis create potential expectations in other areas that need to be recognized and considered?
<--- Score

**53. Are there recognized Telecommunications Analysis problems?**
<--- Score

54. As a sponsor, customer or management, how important is it to meet goals, objectives?
<--- Score

**55. How many trainings, in total, are needed?**
<--- Score

56. Who needs budgets?
<--- Score

57. What resources or support might you need?
<--- Score

58. What needs to be done?
<--- Score

59. What are the Telecommunications Analysis resources needed?
<--- Score

**60. Which information does the Telecommunications Analysis business case need**

**to include?**
<--- Score

61. What should be considered when identifying available resources, constraints, and deadlines?
<--- Score

**62. Do you have/need 24-hour access to key personnel?**
<--- Score

63. How much are sponsors, customers, partners, stakeholders involved in Telecommunications Analysis? In other words, what are the risks, if Telecommunications Analysis does not deliver successfully?
<--- Score

64. What are your needs in relation to Telecommunications Analysis skills, labor, equipment, and markets?
<--- Score

65. Do you know what you need to know about Telecommunications Analysis?
<--- Score

66. What is the problem and/or vulnerability?
<--- Score

67. How can auditing be a preventative security measure?
<--- Score

68. How are the Telecommunications Analysis's objectives aligned to the group's overall stakeholder

strategy?
<--- Score

69. How do you identify subcontractor relationships?
<--- Score

70. What problems are you facing and how do you consider Telecommunications Analysis will circumvent those obstacles?
<--- Score

**71. Are there regulatory / compliance issues?**
<--- Score

72. What are the timeframes required to resolve each of the issues/problems?
<--- Score

73. Consider your own Telecommunications Analysis project, what types of organizational problems do you think might be causing or affecting your problem, based on the work done so far?
<--- Score

74. Will it solve real problems?
<--- Score

**75. What Telecommunications Analysis events should you attend?**
<--- Score

**76. Are employees recognized or rewarded for performance that demonstrates the highest levels of integrity?**
<--- Score

77. To what extent would your organization benefit from being recognized as a award recipient?
<--- Score

78. What is the extent or complexity of the Telecommunications Analysis problem?
<--- Score

79. What activities does the governance board need to consider?
<--- Score

80. Which needs are not included or involved?
<--- Score

**81. Does the problem have ethical dimensions?**
<--- Score

**82. What tools and technologies are needed for a custom Telecommunications Analysis project?**
<--- Score

83. What situation(s) led to this Telecommunications Analysis Self Assessment?
<--- Score

84. What are the minority interests and what amount of minority interests can be recognized?
<--- Score

**85. Why the need?**
<--- Score

86. What would happen if Telecommunications Analysis weren't done?
<--- Score

**87. Do you need different information or graphics?**
<--- Score

88. What Telecommunications Analysis capabilities do you need?
<--- Score

**89. Are you dealing with any of the same issues today as yesterday? What can you do about this?**
<--- Score

90. What are the stakeholder objectives to be achieved with Telecommunications Analysis?
<--- Score

91. Who needs to know?
<--- Score

92. What are the expected benefits of Telecommunications Analysis to the stakeholder?
<--- Score

93. Why is this needed?
<--- Score

94. What training and capacity building actions are needed to implement proposed reforms?
<--- Score

**95. What Telecommunications Analysis coordination do you need?**
<--- Score

**96. For your Telecommunications Analysis project, identify and describe the business environment,**

**is there more than one layer to the business environment?**

<--- Score

97. Do you need to avoid or amend any Telecommunications Analysis activities?

<--- Score

Add up total points for this section:
_ _ _ _ _ = Total points for this section

Divided by: _ _ _ _ _ _ (number of statements answered) = _ _ _ _ _ _
Average score for this section

Transfer your score to the Telecommunications Analysis Index at the beginning of the Self-Assessment.

# CRITERION #2: DEFINE:

INTENT: Formulate the stakeholder problem. Define the problem, needs and objectives.

In my belief, the answer to this question is clearly defined:

5 Strongly Agree

4 Agree

3 Neutral

2 Disagree

1 Strongly Disagree

**1. Is the scope of Telecommunications Analysis defined?**
<--- Score

2. Is the current 'as is' process being followed? If not, what are the discrepancies?
<--- Score

3. If substitutes have been appointed, have they

been briefed on the Telecommunications Analysis goals and received regular communications as to the progress to date?

<--- Score

4. Are approval levels defined for contracts and supplements to contracts?

<--- Score

5. What are the compelling stakeholder reasons for embarking on Telecommunications Analysis?

<--- Score

**6. What is in the scope and what is not in scope?**

<--- Score

7. How do you catch Telecommunications Analysis definition inconsistencies?

<--- Score

8. Is the Telecommunications Analysis scope manageable?

<--- Score

**9. What are the tasks and definitions?**

<--- Score

10. How would you define Telecommunications Analysis leadership?

<--- Score

11. Scope of sensitive information?

<--- Score

12. Are task requirements clearly defined?

<--- Score

13. Has the direction changed at all during the course of Telecommunications Analysis? If so, when did it change and why?
<--- Score

14. Has your scope been defined?
<--- Score

15. Is Telecommunications Analysis required?
<--- Score

16. Are accountability and ownership for Telecommunications Analysis clearly defined?
<--- Score

**17. Are resources adequate for the scope?**
<--- Score

18. Is there regularly 100% attendance at the team meetings? If not, have appointed substitutes attended to preserve cross-functionality and full representation?
<--- Score

**19. Is the Telecommunications Analysis scope complete and appropriately sized?**
<--- Score

**20. How do you manage scope?**
<--- Score

21. How was the 'as is' process map developed, reviewed, verified and validated?
<--- Score

22. What defines best in class?
<--- Score

23. What is the context?
<--- Score

24. Is there any additional Telecommunications Analysis definition of success?
<--- Score

25. How do you manage changes in Telecommunications Analysis requirements?
<--- Score

26. What critical content must be communicated – who, what, when, where, and how?
<--- Score

27. When is/was the Telecommunications Analysis start date?
<--- Score

28. Is scope creep really all bad news?
<--- Score

29. What constraints exist that might impact the team?
<--- Score

**30. What are the requirements for audit information?**
<--- Score

31. Is there a completed SIPOC representation, describing the Suppliers, Inputs, Process, Outputs, and Customers?

<--- Score

32. Do you have organizational privacy requirements?
<--- Score

33. What specifically is the problem? Where does it occur? When does it occur? What is its extent?
<--- Score

34. Has the improvement team collected the 'voice of the customer' (obtained feedback – qualitative and quantitative)?
<--- Score

35. Has a team charter been developed and communicated?
<--- Score

36. What are the boundaries of the scope? What is in bounds and what is not? What is the start point? What is the stop point?
<--- Score

37. Do the problem and goal statements meet the SMART criteria (specific, measurable, attainable, relevant, and time-bound)?
<--- Score

38. What is out-of-scope initially?
<--- Score

39. Have specific policy objectives been defined?
<--- Score

40. What is in scope?
<--- Score

41. Who is gathering information?
<--- Score

**42. Are the Telecommunications Analysis requirements testable?**
<--- Score

43. Does the team have regular meetings?
<--- Score

**44. How do you hand over Telecommunications Analysis context?**
<--- Score

45. How would you define the culture at your organization, how susceptible is it to Telecommunications Analysis changes?
<--- Score

46. Does the scope remain the same?
<--- Score

47. Do you all define Telecommunications Analysis in the same way?
<--- Score

48. When are meeting minutes sent out? Who is on the distribution list?
<--- Score

49. What is the scope?
<--- Score

50. Where can you gather more information?
<--- Score

51. What would be the goal or target for a Telecommunications Analysis's improvement team?
<--- Score

52. Why are you doing Telecommunications Analysis and what is the scope?
<--- Score

53. What customer feedback methods were used to solicit their input?
<--- Score

54. What are the dynamics of the communication plan?
<--- Score

55. What key stakeholder process output measure(s) does Telecommunications Analysis leverage and how?
<--- Score

56. How does the Telecommunications Analysis manager ensure against scope creep?
<--- Score

57. How will the Telecommunications Analysis team and the group measure complete success of Telecommunications Analysis?
<--- Score

58. Has a project plan, Gantt chart, or similar been developed/completed?
<--- Score

59. Are all requirements met?
<--- Score

**60. What gets examined?**

<--- Score

61. How did the Telecommunications Analysis manager receive input to the development of a Telecommunications Analysis improvement plan and the estimated completion dates/times of each activity?

<--- Score

**62. What is the scope of the Telecommunications Analysis work?**

<--- Score

63. What Telecommunications Analysis services do you require?

<--- Score

64. Who are the Telecommunications Analysis improvement team members, including Management Leads and Coaches?

<--- Score

65. Have the customer needs been translated into specific, measurable requirements? How?

<--- Score

66. Are roles and responsibilities formally defined?

<--- Score

**67. What is the worst case scenario?**

<--- Score

68. Is it clearly defined in and to your organization what you do?

<--- Score

**69. What is out of scope?**
<--- Score

70. What was the context?
<--- Score

71. Has everyone on the team, including the team leaders, been properly trained?
<--- Score

72. Is Telecommunications Analysis linked to key stakeholder goals and objectives?
<--- Score

73. What sources do you use to gather information for a Telecommunications Analysis study?
<--- Score

74. How can the value of Telecommunications Analysis be defined?
<--- Score

**75. What system do you use for gathering Telecommunications Analysis information?**
<--- Score

76. Have all basic functions of Telecommunications Analysis been defined?
<--- Score

77. What information do you gather?
<--- Score

78. What scope do you want your strategy to cover?

<--- Score

79. Are there different segments of customers?
<--- Score

80. In what way can you redefine the criteria of choice clients have in your category in your favor?
<--- Score

**81. What are the Telecommunications Analysis use cases?**
<--- Score

82. Is there a clear Telecommunications Analysis case definition?
<--- Score

83. How do you manage unclear Telecommunications Analysis requirements?
<--- Score

84. The political context: who holds power?
<--- Score

**85. What are the core elements of the Telecommunications Analysis business case?**
<--- Score

86. Has the Telecommunications Analysis work been fairly and/or equitably divided and delegated among team members who are qualified and capable to perform the work? Has everyone contributed?
<--- Score

**87. What Telecommunications Analysis requirements should be gathered?**

<--- Score

88. What is the definition of Telecommunications Analysis excellence?
<--- Score

89. Has a high-level 'as is' process map been completed, verified and validated?
<--- Score

90. Is special Telecommunications Analysis user knowledge required?
<--- Score

91. Is there a Telecommunications Analysis management charter, including stakeholder case, problem and goal statements, scope, milestones, roles and responsibilities, communication plan?
<--- Score

92. Are different versions of process maps needed to account for the different types of inputs?
<--- Score

93. What baselines are required to be defined and managed?
<--- Score

94. What is the scope of Telecommunications Analysis?
<--- Score

95. Is Telecommunications Analysis currently on schedule according to the plan?
<--- Score

96. Is the team adequately staffed with the desired cross-functionality? If not, what additional resources are available to the team?
<--- Score

97. What are the Telecommunications Analysis tasks and definitions?
<--- Score

98. When is the estimated completion date?
<--- Score

99. What information should you gather?
<--- Score

100. Has anyone else (internal or external to the group) attempted to solve this problem or a similar one before? If so, what knowledge can be leveraged from these previous efforts?
<--- Score

101. How often are the team meetings?
<--- Score

**102. What intelligence can you gather?**
<--- Score

103. How is the team tracking and documenting its work?
<--- Score

**104. Have all of the relationships been defined properly?**
<--- Score

105. How do you think the partners involved in

Telecommunications Analysis would have defined success?
<--- Score

106. What is the definition of success?
<--- Score

107. Is the improvement team aware of the different versions of a process: what they think it is vs. what it actually is vs. what it should be vs. what it could be?
<--- Score

108. How are consistent Telecommunications Analysis definitions important?
<--- Score

109. What are the Roles and Responsibilities for each team member and its leadership? Where is this documented?
<--- Score

110. Will a Telecommunications Analysis production readiness review be required?
<--- Score

111. How do you keep key subject matter experts in the loop?
<--- Score

112. Is there a critical path to deliver Telecommunications Analysis results?
<--- Score

113. What sort of initial information to gather?
<--- Score

114. How and when will the baselines be defined?
<--- Score

115. Who defines (or who defined) the rules and roles?
<--- Score

116. What are (control) requirements for Telecommunications Analysis Information?
<--- Score

117. Do you have a Telecommunications Analysis success story or case study ready to tell and share?
<--- Score

**118. Are the Telecommunications Analysis requirements complete?**
<--- Score

**119. How do you gather requirements?**
<--- Score

**120. What are the record-keeping requirements of Telecommunications Analysis activities?**
<--- Score

121. How will variation in the actual durations of each activity be dealt with to ensure that the expected Telecommunications Analysis results are met?
<--- Score

122. Are there any constraints known that bear on the ability to perform Telecommunications Analysis work? How is the team addressing them?
<--- Score

123. Is there a completed, verified, and validated high-

level 'as is' (not 'should be' or 'could be') stakeholder process map?
<--- Score

124. What scope to assess?
<--- Score

125. Who approved the Telecommunications Analysis scope?
<--- Score

126. What are the rough order estimates on cost savings/opportunities that Telecommunications Analysis brings?
<--- Score

**127. What is a worst-case scenario for losses?**
<--- Score

128. How do you gather Telecommunications Analysis requirements?
<--- Score

129. Has/have the customer(s) been identified?
<--- Score

**130. How have you defined all Telecommunications Analysis requirements first?**
<--- Score

Add up total points for this section:
_ _ _ _ _ = Total points for this section

Divided by: _ _ _ _ _ _ (number of statements answered) = _ _ _ _ _ _
Average score for this section

Transfer your score to the
Telecommunications Analysis Index at
the beginning of the Self-Assessment.

# CRITERION #3: MEASURE:

INTENT: Gather the correct data.
Measure the current performance and
evolution of the situation.

In my belief, the answer to this
question is clearly defined:

5 Strongly Agree

4 Agree

3 Neutral

2 Disagree

1 Strongly Disagree

1. How will your organization measure success?
<--- Score

**2. What happens if cost savings do not materialize?**
<--- Score

**3. Who pays the cost?**
<--- Score

4. When are costs are incurred?

<--- Score

**5. Where is the cost?**

<--- Score

6. What are hidden Telecommunications Analysis quality costs?

<--- Score

**7. What is measured? Why?**

<--- Score

**8. How sensitive must the Telecommunications Analysis strategy be to cost?**

<--- Score

**9. How do you verify and validate the Telecommunications Analysis data?**

<--- Score

10. When should you bother with diagrams?

<--- Score

11. Does management have the right priorities among projects?

<--- Score

12. What causes extra work or rework?

<--- Score

**13. How do you verify the Telecommunications Analysis requirements quality?**

<--- Score

14. Where can you go to verify the info?

<--- Score

15. How is progress measured?
<--- Score

**16. How will costs be allocated?**
<--- Score

**17. Have design-to-cost goals been established?**
<--- Score

18. Which costs should be taken into account?
<--- Score

19. What are the Telecommunications Analysis key cost drivers?
<--- Score

20. How to cause the change?
<--- Score

**21. What are the estimated costs of proposed changes?**
<--- Score

**22. How do you verify performance?**
<--- Score

**23. Are actual costs in line with budgeted costs?**
<--- Score

24. What causes investor action?
<--- Score

25. Are Telecommunications Analysis vulnerabilities categorized and prioritized?

<--- Score

26. How will success or failure be measured?
<--- Score

**27. What does your operating model cost?**
<--- Score

**28. How do you prevent mis-estimating cost?**
<--- Score

29. How is the value delivered by Telecommunications Analysis being measured?
<--- Score

30. Are there competing Telecommunications Analysis priorities?
<--- Score

31. Do you effectively measure and reward individual and team performance?
<--- Score

32. Are the Telecommunications Analysis benefits worth its costs?
<--- Score

**33. What are your operating costs?**
<--- Score

34. Do the benefits outweigh the costs?
<--- Score

**35. What are the types and number of measures to use?**
<--- Score

36. How can you reduce costs?
<--- Score

37. Did you tackle the cause or the symptom?
<--- Score

**38. Do you have a flow diagram of what happens?**
<--- Score

39. How long to keep data and how to manage
retention costs?
<--- Score

**40. Is the solution cost-effective?**
<--- Score

41. What are your key Telecommunications Analysis
organizational performance measures, including key
short and longer-term financial measures?
<--- Score

42. Are you able to realize any cost savings?
<--- Score

43. Have you included everything in your
Telecommunications Analysis cost models?
<--- Score

44. Which measures and indicators matter?
<--- Score

45. What users will be impacted?
<--- Score

46. Among the Telecommunications Analysis product

and service cost to be estimated, which is considered hardest to estimate?

<--- Score

47. How can a Telecommunications Analysis test verify your ideas or assumptions?

<--- Score

48. What are the strategic priorities for this year?

<--- Score

49. What is the total cost related to deploying Telecommunications Analysis, including any consulting or professional services?

<--- Score

50. What are the uncertainties surrounding estimates of impact?

<--- Score

51. Are you taking your company in the direction of better and revenue or cheaper and cost?

<--- Score

52. How are measurements made?

<--- Score

53. At what cost?

<--- Score

54. What is the root cause(s) of the problem?

<--- Score

55. Are there any easy-to-implement alternatives to Telecommunications Analysis? Sometimes other solutions are available that do not require the cost

implications of a full-blown project?

<--- Score

**56. What potential environmental factors impact the Telecommunications Analysis effort?**

<--- Score

57. How frequently do you track Telecommunications Analysis measures?

<--- Score

**58. How do you verify the authenticity of the data and information used?**

<--- Score

59. Where is it measured?

<--- Score

60. What are the Telecommunications Analysis investment costs?

<--- Score

61. Have you made assumptions about the shape of the future, particularly its impact on your customers and competitors?

<--- Score

**62. What methods are feasible and acceptable to estimate the impact of reforms?**

<--- Score

63. How do you control the overall costs of your work processes?

<--- Score

64. How do you measure efficient delivery of

Telecommunications Analysis services?
<--- Score

65. Are the measurements objective?
<--- Score

66. Why do you expend time and effort to implement measurement, for whom?
<--- Score

**67. How do you aggregate measures across priorities?**
<--- Score

**68. Are there measurements based on task performance?**
<--- Score

69. Who should receive measurement reports?
<--- Score

70. What do people want to verify?
<--- Score

**71. What do you measure and why?**
<--- Score

72. What measurements are being captured?
<--- Score

73. Will Telecommunications Analysis have an impact on current business continuity, disaster recovery processes and/or infrastructure?
<--- Score

**74. When a disaster occurs, who gets priority?**

<--- Score

## 75. How is performance measured?
<--- Score

76. What is the cause of any Telecommunications Analysis gaps?
<--- Score

77. What can be used to verify compliance?
<--- Score

## 78. What causes innovation to fail or succeed in your organization?
<--- Score

## 79. How can you reduce the costs of obtaining inputs?
<--- Score

80. What are the costs?
<--- Score

81. What are the operational costs after Telecommunications Analysis deployment?
<--- Score

## 82. Do you have an issue in getting priority?
<--- Score

## 83. Was a business case (cost/benefit) developed?
<--- Score

84. How do you measure success?
<--- Score

85. Are indirect costs charged to the Telecommunications Analysis program?
<--- Score

**86. Do you aggressively reward and promote the people who have the biggest impact on creating excellent Telecommunications Analysis services/ products?**
<--- Score

87. What would be a real cause for concern?
<--- Score

88. What tests verify requirements?
<--- Score

**89. How much does it cost?**
<--- Score

90. What is your decision requirements diagram?
<--- Score

91. Is there an opportunity to verify requirements?
<--- Score

**92. What is the cost of rework?**
<--- Score

93. How do you verify if Telecommunications Analysis is built right?
<--- Score

94. How do you quantify and qualify impacts?
<--- Score

**95. Are supply costs steady or fluctuating?**

<--- Score

96. What are your primary costs, revenues, assets?
<--- Score

**97. Which Telecommunications Analysis impacts are significant?**
<--- Score

98. Does the Telecommunications Analysis task fit the client's priorities?
<--- Score

99. What are the costs of reform?
<--- Score

**100. How do you measure lifecycle phases?**
<--- Score

101. What is the total fixed cost?
<--- Score

102. What are you verifying?
<--- Score

103. How do you verify and develop ideas and innovations?
<--- Score

104. What does a Test Case verify?
<--- Score

105. What measurements are possible, practicable and meaningful?
<--- Score

106. How will you measure your Telecommunications Analysis effectiveness?
<--- Score

107. How can you manage cost down?
<--- Score

108. What harm might be caused?
<--- Score

**109. What does verifying compliance entail?**
<--- Score

110. Has a cost center been established?
<--- Score

111. What does losing customers cost your organization?
<--- Score

**112. What causes mismanagement?**
<--- Score

113. What evidence is there and what is measured?
<--- Score

114. What would it cost to replace your technology?
<--- Score

115. What are the costs of delaying Telecommunications Analysis action?
<--- Score

116. How will you measure success?
<--- Score

117. Are the units of measure consistent?
<--- Score

118. Does a Telecommunications Analysis quantification method exist?
<--- Score

119. Is it possible to estimate the impact of unanticipated complexity such as wrong or failed assumptions, feedback, etcetera on proposed reforms?
<--- Score

120. What are the costs and benefits?
<--- Score

121. How do you verify Telecommunications Analysis completeness and accuracy?
<--- Score

122. How do you measure variability?
<--- Score

123. How can you measure the performance?
<--- Score

**124. What relevant entities could be measured?**
<--- Score

125. How do your measurements capture actionable Telecommunications Analysis information for use in exceeding your customers expectations and securing your customers engagement?
<--- Score

126. What is your Telecommunications Analysis

quality cost segregation study?
<--- Score

127. What is the Telecommunications Analysis
business impact?
<--- Score

128. What are allowable costs?
<--- Score

129. What disadvantage does this cause for the user?
<--- Score

**130. Who is involved in verifying compliance?**
<--- Score

**131. What drives O&M cost?**
<--- Score

**132. How will effects be measured?**
<--- Score

**133. Are missed Telecommunications Analysis
opportunities costing your organization money?**
<--- Score

134. How are costs allocated?
<--- Score

135. What is an unallowable cost?
<--- Score

Add up total points for this section:
_ _ _ _ _  = Total points for this section

Divided by: _ _ _ _ _ _  (number of

statements answered) =  _____
Average score for this section

Transfer your score to the
Telecommunications Analysis Index at
the beginning of the Self-Assessment.

# CRITERION #4: ANALYZE:

INTENT: Analyze causes, assumptions and hypotheses.

In my belief, the answer to this question is clearly defined:

5 Strongly Agree

4 Agree

3 Neutral

2 Disagree

1 Strongly Disagree

**1. Think about the functions involved in your Telecommunications Analysis project, what processes flow from these functions?**
<--- Score

**2. How do you identify specific Telecommunications Analysis investment opportunities and emerging trends?**
<--- Score

3. What are the Telecommunications Analysis design outputs?
<--- Score

4. Do your employees have the opportunity to do what they do best everyday?
<--- Score

5. Who will gather what data?
<--- Score

6. What output to create?
<--- Score

7. Was a detailed process map created to amplify critical steps of the 'as is' stakeholder process?
<--- Score

8. What successful thing are you doing today that may be blinding you to new growth opportunities?
<--- Score

9. Did any additional data need to be collected?
<--- Score

**10. What qualifications and skills do you need?**
<--- Score

11. How do you use Telecommunications Analysis data and information to support organizational decision making and innovation?
<--- Score

12. Is there any way to speed up the process?
<--- Score

13. What are your current levels and trends in key Telecommunications Analysis measures or indicators of product and process performance that are important to and directly serve your customers?
<--- Score

14. What resources go in to get the desired output?
<--- Score

15. Where is Telecommunications Analysis data gathered?
<--- Score

16. Is data and process analysis, root cause analysis and quantifying the gap/opportunity in place?
<--- Score

17. What qualifications are necessary?
<--- Score

18. Do staff qualifications match your project?
<--- Score

**19. Where is the data coming from to measure compliance?**
<--- Score

20. How difficult is it to qualify what Telecommunications Analysis ROI is?
<--- Score

21. When should a process be art not science?
<--- Score

22. How will the change process be managed?
<--- Score

**23. A compounding model resolution with available relevant data can often provide insight towards a solution methodology; which Telecommunications Analysis models, tools and techniques are necessary?**

<--- Score

**24. What methods do you use to gather Telecommunications Analysis data?**

<--- Score

25. What types of data do your Telecommunications Analysis indicators require?

<--- Score

26. What will drive Telecommunications Analysis change?

<--- Score

27. What are your key performance measures or indicators and in-process measures for the control and improvement of your Telecommunications Analysis processes?

<--- Score

28. How many input/output points does it require?

<--- Score

**29. An organizationally feasible system request is one that considers the mission, goals and objectives of the organization, key questions are: is the Telecommunications Analysis solution request practical and will it solve a problem or take advantage of an opportunity to achieve company goals?**

<--- Score

**30. What kind of crime could a potential new hire have committed that would not only not disqualify him/her from being hired by your organization, but would actually indicate that he/she might be a particularly good fit?**
<--- Score

**31. How do you promote understanding that opportunity for improvement is not criticism of the status quo, or the people who created the status quo?**
<--- Score

32. How do you define collaboration and team output?
<--- Score

33. How has the Telecommunications Analysis data been gathered?
<--- Score

**34. Do you have the authority to produce the output?**
<--- Score

35. Are gaps between current performance and the goal performance identified?
<--- Score

36. Have you defined which data is gathered how?
<--- Score

37. What are the revised rough estimates of the financial savings/opportunity for Telecommunications

Analysis improvements?

<--- Score

38. Can you add value to the current Telecommunications Analysis decision-making process (largely qualitative) by incorporating uncertainty modeling (more quantitative)?

<--- Score

39. How does the organization define, manage, and improve its Telecommunications Analysis processes?

<--- Score

40. What were the crucial 'moments of truth' on the process map?

<--- Score

**41. Do quality systems drive continuous improvement?**

<--- Score

**42. How much data can be collected in the given timeframe?**

<--- Score

43. Is the required Telecommunications Analysis data gathered?

<--- Score

**44. How is the Telecommunications Analysis Value Stream Mapping managed?**

<--- Score

45. How is data used for program management and improvement?

<--- Score

46. What are your outputs?
<--- Score

**47. How do you implement and manage your work processes to ensure that they meet design requirements?**
<--- Score

48. What are the processes for audit reporting and management?
<--- Score

49. What, related to, Telecommunications Analysis processes does your organization outsource?
<--- Score

50. How are outputs preserved and protected?
<--- Score

**51. Which Telecommunications Analysis data should be retained?**
<--- Score

52. What were the financial benefits resulting from any 'ground fruit or low-hanging fruit' (quick fixes)?
<--- Score

53. What are the necessary qualifications?
<--- Score

**54. What are the personnel training and qualifications required?**
<--- Score

**55. What data is gathered?**

<--- Score

56. Who gets your output?
<--- Score

57. Who is involved with workflow mapping?
<--- Score

58. What is the output?
<--- Score

59. What controls do you have in place to protect data?
<--- Score

60. Is the gap/opportunity displayed and communicated in financial terms?
<--- Score

61. What are your best practices for minimizing Telecommunications Analysis project risk, while demonstrating incremental value and quick wins throughout the Telecommunications Analysis project lifecycle?
<--- Score

62. What qualifies as competition?
<--- Score

63. Do several people in different organizational units assist with the Telecommunications Analysis process?
<--- Score

64. Were any designed experiments used to generate additional insight into the data analysis?
<--- Score

65. Did any value-added analysis or 'lean thinking' take place to identify some of the gaps shown on the 'as is' process map?
<--- Score

**66. What other organizational variables, such as reward systems or communication systems, affect the performance of this Telecommunications Analysis process?**
<--- Score

67. Have any additional benefits been identified that will result from closing all or most of the gaps?
<--- Score

68. Has data output been validated?
<--- Score

69. What systems/processes must you excel at?
<--- Score

**70. What are your Telecommunications Analysis processes?**
<--- Score

71. Do you, as a leader, bounce back quickly from setbacks?
<--- Score

72. What tools were used to narrow the list of possible causes?
<--- Score

73. What does the data say about the performance of the stakeholder process?

<--- Score

74. What is the cost of poor quality as supported by the team's analysis?
<--- Score

**75. Are you missing Telecommunications Analysis opportunities?**
<--- Score

76. What is your organizations system for selecting qualified vendors?
<--- Score

77. Think about some of the processes you undertake within your organization, which do you own?
<--- Score

78. What Telecommunications Analysis data should be managed?
<--- Score

79. Do you understand your management processes today?
<--- Score

80. Are all staff in core Telecommunications Analysis subjects Highly Qualified?
<--- Score

81. What are the Telecommunications Analysis business drivers?
<--- Score

**82. What is the complexity of the output produced?**

<--- Score

83. What tools were used to generate the list of possible causes?
<--- Score

84. Do your contracts/agreements contain data security obligations?
<--- Score

**85. How do you ensure that the Telecommunications Analysis opportunity is realistic?**
<--- Score

86. Was a cause-and-effect diagram used to explore the different types of causes (or sources of variation)?
<--- Score

87. Where can you get qualified talent today?
<--- Score

**88. What are the best opportunities for value improvement?**
<--- Score

89. How is the way you as the leader think and process information affecting your organizational culture?
<--- Score

90. Is pre-qualification of suppliers carried out?
<--- Score

91. What did the team gain from developing a sub-process map?
<--- Score

92. Is the final output clearly identified?
<--- Score

93. Identify an operational issue in your organization, for example, could a particular task be done more quickly or more efficiently by Telecommunications Analysis?
<--- Score

94. What Telecommunications Analysis data do you gather or use now?
<--- Score

95. Who is involved in the management review process?
<--- Score

96. What are your current levels and trends in key measures or indicators of Telecommunications Analysis product and process performance that are important to and directly serve your customers? How do these results compare with the performance of your competitors and other organizations with similar offerings?
<--- Score

97. Is the suppliers process defined and controlled?
<--- Score

98. Are Telecommunications Analysis changes recognized early enough to be approved through the regular process?
<--- Score

99. Is the Telecommunications Analysis process

severely broken such that a re-design is necessary?
<--- Score

100. How often will data be collected for measures?
<--- Score

101. Has an output goal been set?
<--- Score

**102. What training and qualifications will you need?**
<--- Score

103. What quality tools were used to get through the analyze phase?
<--- Score

104. What process improvements will be needed?
<--- Score

105. What are evaluation criteria for the output?
<--- Score

106. Have the problem and goal statements been updated to reflect the additional knowledge gained from the analyze phase?
<--- Score

107. How will the Telecommunications Analysis data be captured?
<--- Score

108. Do your leaders quickly bounce back from setbacks?
<--- Score

109. What qualifications do Telecommunications Analysis leaders need?

<--- Score

**110. What is your organizations process which leads to recognition of value generation?**

<--- Score

111. What Telecommunications Analysis data should be collected?

<--- Score

112. Who qualifies to gain access to data?

<--- Score

113. Is the performance gap determined?

<--- Score

114. What is the oversight process?

<--- Score

115. What internal processes need improvement?

<--- Score

116. Are your outputs consistent?

<--- Score

117. Is there an established change management process?

<--- Score

118. What are the disruptive Telecommunications Analysis technologies that enable your organization to radically change your business processes?

<--- Score

119. What is the Value Stream Mapping?
<--- Score

120. What is the Telecommunications Analysis Driver?
<--- Score

**121. What qualifications are needed?**
<--- Score

122. Were Pareto charts (or similar) used to portray the 'heavy hitters' (or key sources of variation)?
<--- Score

123. How is the data gathered?
<--- Score

124. How do your work systems and key work processes relate to and capitalize on your core competencies?
<--- Score

125. What conclusions were drawn from the team's data collection and analysis? How did the team reach these conclusions?
<--- Score

126. What do you need to qualify?
<--- Score

127. Is there a strict change management process?
<--- Score

128. How is Telecommunications Analysis data gathered?
<--- Score

129. Were there any improvement opportunities identified from the process analysis?
<--- Score

130. How was the detailed process map generated, verified, and validated?
<--- Score

Add up total points for this section:
_ _ _ _ _ = Total points for this section

Divided by: _ _ _ _ _ _ (number of statements answered) = _ _ _ _ _ _
Average score for this section

Transfer your score to the Telecommunications Analysis Index at the beginning of the Self-Assessment.

# CRITERION #5: IMPROVE:

INTENT: Develop a practical solution. Innovate, establish and test the solution and to measure the results.

In my belief, the answer to this question is clearly defined:

5 Strongly Agree

4 Agree

3 Neutral

2 Disagree

1 Strongly Disagree

1. What is the Telecommunications Analysis's sustainability risk?
<--- Score

**2. How can you better manage risk?**
<--- Score

3. What assumptions are made about the solution and approach?

<--- Score

4. If you could go back in time five years, what decision would you make differently? What is your best guess as to what decision you're making today you might regret five years from now?
<--- Score

5. What are your current levels and trends in key measures or indicators of workforce and leader development?
<--- Score

6. Where do the Telecommunications Analysis decisions reside?
<--- Score

7. Where do you need Telecommunications Analysis improvement?
<--- Score

8. For estimation problems, how do you develop an estimation statement?
<--- Score

9. Was a Telecommunications Analysis charter developed?
<--- Score

10. Would you develop a Telecommunications Analysis Communication Strategy?
<--- Score

11. How is knowledge sharing about risk management improved?
<--- Score

12. Is Telecommunications Analysis documentation maintained?
<--- Score

13. Will the controls trigger any other risks?
<--- Score

14. How do you mitigate Telecommunications Analysis risk?
<--- Score

**15. Who makes the Telecommunications Analysis decisions in your organization?**
<--- Score

**16. How does your organization evaluate strategic Telecommunications Analysis success?**
<--- Score

17. Telecommunications Analysis risk decisions: whose call Is It?
<--- Score

**18. What were the criteria for evaluating a Telecommunications Analysis pilot?**
<--- Score

**19. How can skill-level changes improve Telecommunications Analysis?**
<--- Score

20. How can the phases of Telecommunications Analysis development be identified?
<--- Score

21. Who are the key stakeholders for the Telecommunications Analysis evaluation?
<--- Score

22. What error proofing will be done to address some of the discrepancies observed in the 'as is' process?
<--- Score

23. Is the solution technically practical?
<--- Score

24. How risky is your organization?
<--- Score

25. Who controls key decisions that will be made?
<--- Score

**26. Is the Telecommunications Analysis risk managed?**
<--- Score

27. Was a pilot designed for the proposed solution(s)?
<--- Score

28. Which of the recognised risks out of all risks can be most likely transferred?
<--- Score

**29. Who do you report Telecommunications Analysis results to?**
<--- Score

30. How do you keep improving Telecommunications Analysis?
<--- Score

31. Explorations of the frontiers of Telecommunications Analysis will help you build influence, improve Telecommunications Analysis, optimize decision making, and sustain change, what is your approach?
<--- Score

32. How scalable is your Telecommunications Analysis solution?
<--- Score

33. How are policy decisions made and where?
<--- Score

34. What risks do you need to manage?
<--- Score

35. Which Telecommunications Analysis solution is appropriate?
<--- Score

**36. How can you improve Telecommunications Analysis?**
<--- Score

37. Is the implementation plan designed?
<--- Score

38. What is the magnitude of the improvements?
<--- Score

39. What went well, what should change, what can improve?
<--- Score

**40. To what extent does management recognize**

**Telecommunications Analysis as a tool to increase the results?**

<--- Score

41. Are you assessing Telecommunications Analysis and risk?

<--- Score

42. Is there any other Telecommunications Analysis solution?

<--- Score

43. How do you manage Telecommunications Analysis risk?

<--- Score

44. What is the implementation plan?

<--- Score

45. Is supporting Telecommunications Analysis documentation required?

<--- Score

**46. What needs improvement? Why?**

<--- Score

**47. Does a good decision guarantee a good outcome?**

<--- Score

48. Have you identified breakpoints and/or risk tolerances that will trigger broad consideration of a potential need for intervention or modification of strategy?

<--- Score

**49. Is the scope clearly documented?**

<--- Score

50. Risk events: what are the things that could go wrong?

<--- Score

51. What are the implications of the one critical Telecommunications Analysis decision 10 minutes, 10 months, and 10 years from now?

<--- Score

52. What is the risk?

<--- Score

53. What practices helps your organization to develop its capacity to recognize patterns?

<--- Score

**54. Do you need to do a usability evaluation?**

<--- Score

55. What tools were most useful during the improve phase?

<--- Score

56. How do you measure improved Telecommunications Analysis service perception, and satisfaction?

<--- Score

57. Who manages Telecommunications Analysis risk?

<--- Score

**58. How risky is your organization?**

<--- Score

59. Is the measure of success for Telecommunications Analysis understandable to a variety of people?
<--- Score

60. Are decisions made in a timely manner?
<--- Score

61. For decision problems, how do you develop a decision statement?
<--- Score

62. Are the most efficient solutions problem-specific?
<--- Score

63. What Telecommunications Analysis improvements can be made?
<--- Score

**64. How do you go about comparing Telecommunications Analysis approaches/ solutions?**
<--- Score

65. What lessons, if any, from a pilot were incorporated into the design of the full-scale solution?
<--- Score

66. Is the Telecommunications Analysis solution sustainable?
<--- Score

67. Are events managed to resolution?
<--- Score

68. In the past few months, what is the smallest

change you have made that has had the biggest positive result? What was it about that small change that produced the large return?
<--- Score

**69. Do you combine technical expertise with business knowledge and Telecommunications Analysis Key topics include lifecycles, development approaches, requirements and how to make a business case?**
<--- Score

70. What attendant changes will need to be made to ensure that the solution is successful?
<--- Score

71. Can you integrate quality management and risk management?
<--- Score

72. Do vendor agreements bring new compliance risk ?
<--- Score

73. Who are the Telecommunications Analysis decision makers?
<--- Score

74. What does the 'should be' process map/design look like?
<--- Score

75. How do you improve your likelihood of success ?
<--- Score

76. Who will be using the results of the measurement

activities?

<--- Score

**77. How do you improve Telecommunications Analysis service perception, and satisfaction?**

<--- Score

78. Is there a small-scale pilot for proposed improvement(s)? What conclusions were drawn from the outcomes of a pilot?

<--- Score

79. Who controls the risk?

<--- Score

80. Is there a cost/benefit analysis of optimal solution(s)?

<--- Score

81. What to do with the results or outcomes of measurements?

<--- Score

82. How will you measure the results?

<--- Score

83. Risk Identification: What are the possible risk events your organization faces in relation to Telecommunications Analysis?

<--- Score

84. What are the expected Telecommunications Analysis results?

<--- Score

85. How do you decide how much to remunerate an

employee?
<--- Score

86. What are the Telecommunications Analysis
security risks?
<--- Score

87. Who are the people involved in developing and
implementing Telecommunications Analysis?
<--- Score

88. Do those selected for the Telecommunications
Analysis team have a good general understanding of
what Telecommunications Analysis is all about?
<--- Score

**89. What tools do you use once you have decided
on a Telecommunications Analysis strategy and
more importantly how do you choose?**
<--- Score

**90. How will you know that a change is an
improvement?**
<--- Score

**91. Have you achieved Telecommunications
Analysis improvements?**
<--- Score

**92. How does the team improve its work?**
<--- Score

93. What strategies for Telecommunications Analysis
improvement are successful?
<--- Score

94. Are risk management tasks balanced centrally and locally?
<--- Score

95. How can you improve performance?
<--- Score

96. How are Telecommunications Analysis risks managed?
<--- Score

97. What is Telecommunications Analysis risk?
<--- Score

98. What were the underlying assumptions on the cost-benefit analysis?
<--- Score

**99. At what point will vulnerability assessments be performed once Telecommunications Analysis is put into production (e.g., ongoing Risk Management after implementation)?**
<--- Score

**100. Does the goal represent a desired result that can be measured?**
<--- Score

**101. Is any Telecommunications Analysis documentation required?**
<--- Score

102. How do you deal with Telecommunications Analysis risk?
<--- Score

103. What improvements have been achieved?
<--- Score

104. Are risk triggers captured?
<--- Score

105. Is the optimal solution selected based on testing and analysis?
<--- Score

106. What are the concrete Telecommunications Analysis results?
<--- Score

107. Can the solution be designed and implemented within an acceptable time period?
<--- Score

**108. How do you manage and improve your Telecommunications Analysis work systems to deliver customer value and achieve organizational success and sustainability?**
<--- Score

109. What area needs the greatest improvement?
<--- Score

110. What tools were used to evaluate the potential solutions?
<--- Score

111. What is Telecommunications Analysis's impact on utilizing the best solution(s)?
<--- Score

112. How do you define the solutions' scope?

<--- Score

113. Risk factors: what are the characteristics of Telecommunications Analysis that make it risky?
<--- Score

114. What tools were used to tap into the creativity and encourage 'outside the box' thinking?
<--- Score

**115. How do the Telecommunications Analysis results compare with the performance of your competitors and other organizations with similar offerings?**
<--- Score

**116. What should a proof of concept or pilot accomplish?**
<--- Score

117. Can you identify any significant risks or exposures to Telecommunications Analysis third- parties (vendors, service providers, alliance partners etc) that concern you?
<--- Score

118. What is the team's contingency plan for potential problems occurring in implementation?
<--- Score

119. What are the affordable Telecommunications Analysis risks?
<--- Score

120. How is continuous improvement applied to risk management?

<--- Score

121. How do you measure progress and evaluate training effectiveness?
<--- Score

122. What actually has to improve and by how much?
<--- Score

**123. How will you recognize and celebrate results?**
<--- Score

124. How do you link measurement and risk?
<--- Score

125. Do you cover the five essential competencies: Communication, Collaboration,Innovation, Adaptability, and Leadership that improve an organizations ability to leverage the new Telecommunications Analysis in a volatile global economy?
<--- Score

126. How do you improve productivity?
<--- Score

**127. What criteria will you use to assess your Telecommunications Analysis risks?**
<--- Score

128. What do you want to improve?
<--- Score

129. What communications are necessary to support the implementation of the solution?
<--- Score

130. How will you know that you have improved?
<--- Score

**131. When you map the key players in your own work and the types/domains of relationships with them, which relationships do you find easy and which challenging, and why?**
<--- Score

132. Is risk periodically assessed?
<--- Score

133. Were any criteria developed to assist the team in testing and evaluating potential solutions?
<--- Score

134. Why improve in the first place?
<--- Score

**135. How do you measure risk?**
<--- Score

Add up total points for this section:
_ _ _ _ _ = Total points for this section

Divided by: _ _ _ _ _ _ (number of statements answered) = _ _ _ _ _ _
Average score for this section

Transfer your score to the Telecommunications Analysis Index at the beginning of the Self-Assessment.

# CRITERION #6: CONTROL:

INTENT: Implement the practical solution. Maintain the performance and correct possible complications.

In my belief, the answer to this question is clearly defined:

5 Strongly Agree

4 Agree

3 Neutral

2 Disagree

1 Strongly Disagree

1. How will the process owner verify improvement in present and future sigma levels, process capabilities? <--- Score

2. You may have created your quality measures at a time when you lacked resources, technology wasn't up to the required standard, or low service levels were the industry norm. Have those circumstances changed?

<--- Score

3. What are the known security controls?
<--- Score

4. What quality tools were useful in the control phase?
<--- Score

5. Is knowledge gained on process shared and institutionalized?
<--- Score

6. How do you establish and deploy modified action plans if circumstances require a shift in plans and rapid execution of new plans?
<--- Score

7. Is there a standardized process?
<--- Score

8. What key inputs and outputs are being measured on an ongoing basis?
<--- Score

9. What should you measure to verify efficiency gains?
<--- Score

**10. How do you encourage people to take control and responsibility?**
<--- Score

11. What should the next improvement project be that is related to Telecommunications Analysis?
<--- Score

12. What adjustments to the strategies are needed?

<--- Score

**13. Is there a Telecommunications Analysis Communication plan covering who needs to get what information when?**
<--- Score

14. Do the Telecommunications Analysis decisions you make today help people and the planet tomorrow?
<--- Score

15. Does job training on the documented procedures need to be part of the process team's education and training?
<--- Score

**16. How likely is the current Telecommunications Analysis plan to come in on schedule or on budget?**
<--- Score

17. Does a troubleshooting guide exist or is it needed?
<--- Score

18. How do you plan for the cost of succession?
<--- Score

19. Are the planned controls working?
<--- Score

20. Is a response plan established and deployed?
<--- Score

21. Are there documented procedures?
<--- Score

22. Is there a documented and implemented monitoring plan?

<--- Score

**23. How is change control managed?**

<--- Score

24. Is reporting being used or needed?

<--- Score

**25. Is the Telecommunications Analysis test/ monitoring cost justified?**

<--- Score

**26. What are your results for key measures or indicators of the accomplishment of your Telecommunications Analysis strategy and action plans, including building and strengthening core competencies?**

<--- Score

27. What are the critical parameters to watch?

<--- Score

28. Will your goals reflect your program budget?

<--- Score

**29. Who sets the Telecommunications Analysis standards?**

<--- Score

30. What is the standard for acceptable Telecommunications Analysis performance?

<--- Score

31. Are documented procedures clear and easy to

follow for the operators?

<--- Score

32. Are suggested corrective/restorative actions indicated on the response plan for known causes to problems that might surface?

<--- Score

33. How will report readings be checked to effectively monitor performance?

<--- Score

**34. Are pertinent alerts monitored, analyzed and distributed to appropriate personnel?**

<--- Score

35. Are new process steps, standards, and documentation ingrained into normal operations?

<--- Score

36. Does the Telecommunications Analysis performance meet the customer's requirements?

<--- Score

37. How will the process owner and team be able to hold the gains?

<--- Score

38. Can you adapt and adjust to changing Telecommunications Analysis situations?

<--- Score

39. What is the control/monitoring plan?

<--- Score

40. Are you measuring, monitoring and predicting

Telecommunications Analysis activities to optimize operations and profitability, and enhancing outcomes?
<--- Score

41. Is new knowledge gained imbedded in the response plan?
<--- Score

42. How do you plan on providing proper recognition and disclosure of supporting companies?
<--- Score

**43. Who has control over resources?**
<--- Score

44. What is the recommended frequency of auditing?
<--- Score

45. How will new or emerging customer needs/ requirements be checked/communicated to orient the process toward meeting the new specifications and continually reducing variation?
<--- Score

46. How do you monitor usage and cost?
<--- Score

47. Where do ideas that reach policy makers and planners as proposals for Telecommunications Analysis strengthening and reform actually originate?
<--- Score

48. How do you select, collect, align, and integrate Telecommunications Analysis data and information for tracking daily operations and overall

organizational performance, including progress relative to strategic objectives and action plans?
<--- Score

49. Have new or revised work instructions resulted?
<--- Score

50. What is your theory of human motivation, and how does your compensation plan fit with that view?
<--- Score

51. Is there a control plan in place for sustaining improvements (short and long-term)?
<--- Score

**52. Against what alternative is success being measured?**
<--- Score

**53. How do senior leaders actions reflect a commitment to the organizations Telecommunications Analysis values?**
<--- Score

**54. Who will be in control?**
<--- Score

55. Are controls in place and consistently applied?
<--- Score

56. What Telecommunications Analysis standards are applicable?
<--- Score

57. Will existing staff require re-training, for example, to learn new business processes?

<--- Score

58. Does the response plan contain a definite closed loop continual improvement scheme (e.g., plan-do-check-act)?
<--- Score

**59. Act/Adjust: What Do you Need to Do Differently?**
<--- Score

60. How will input, process, and output variables be checked to detect for sub-optimal conditions?
<--- Score

61. What other areas of the group might benefit from the Telecommunications Analysis team's improvements, knowledge, and learning?
<--- Score

**62. How can you best use all of your knowledge repositories to enhance learning and sharing?**
<--- Score

63. In the case of a Telecommunications Analysis project, the criteria for the audit derive from implementation objectives, an audit of a Telecommunications Analysis project involves assessing whether the recommendations outlined for implementation have been met, can you track that any Telecommunications Analysis project is implemented as planned, and is it working?
<--- Score

64. Do you monitor the Telecommunications Analysis decisions made and fine tune them as they evolve?

<--- Score

65. How do your controls stack up?
<--- Score

66. Does Telecommunications Analysis appropriately measure and monitor risk?
<--- Score

67. Do you monitor the effectiveness of your Telecommunications Analysis activities?
<--- Score

**68. Can support from partners be adjusted?**
<--- Score

**69. Are the planned controls in place?**
<--- Score

70. Is there a recommended audit plan for routine surveillance inspections of Telecommunications Analysis's gains?
<--- Score

71. Implementation Planning: is a pilot needed to test the changes before a full roll out occurs?
<--- Score

72. How will you measure your QA plan's effectiveness?
<--- Score

73. Has the Telecommunications Analysis value of standards been quantified?
<--- Score

74. Has the improved process and its steps been standardized?
<--- Score

75. Are operating procedures consistent?
<--- Score

76. Are the Telecommunications Analysis standards challenging?
<--- Score

77. What is your plan to assess your security risks?
<--- Score

78. Is there documentation that will support the successful operation of the improvement?
<--- Score

79. How is Telecommunications Analysis project cost planned, managed, monitored?
<--- Score

**80. Who is going to spread your message?**
<--- Score

81. Who is the Telecommunications Analysis process owner?
<--- Score

82. Is there a transfer of ownership and knowledge to process owner and process team tasked with the responsibilities.
<--- Score

83. What do you stand for--and what are you against?
<--- Score

84. Who controls critical resources?
<--- Score

**85. What are the key elements of your Telecommunications Analysis performance improvement system, including your evaluation, organizational learning, and innovation processes?**
<--- Score

86. What are customers monitoring?
<--- Score

87. How will Telecommunications Analysis decisions be made and monitored?
<--- Score

88. How will the day-to-day responsibilities for monitoring and continual improvement be transferred from the improvement team to the process owner?
<--- Score

89. How might the group capture best practices and lessons learned so as to leverage improvements?
<--- Score

90. What other systems, operations, processes, and infrastructures (hiring practices, staffing, training, incentives/rewards, metrics/dashboards/scorecards, etc.) need updates, additions, changes, or deletions in order to facilitate knowledge transfer and improvements?
<--- Score

91. Is a response plan in place for when the input, process, or output measures indicate an 'out-of-control' condition?
<--- Score

92. Will any special training be provided for results interpretation?
<--- Score

93. How do you spread information?
<--- Score

94. Will the team be available to assist members in planning investigations?
<--- Score

95. How widespread is its use?
<--- Score

96. How do controls support value?
<--- Score

97. What is the best design framework for Telecommunications Analysis organization now that, in a post industrial-age if the top-down, command and control model is no longer relevant?
<--- Score

98. What do you measure to verify effectiveness gains?
<--- Score

**99. Is there an action plan in case of emergencies?**
<--- Score

100. What are you attempting to measure/monitor?

<--- Score

101. What do your reports reflect?
<--- Score

Add up total points for this section:
_ _ _ _ _ = Total points for this section

Divided by: _ _ _ _ _ _ (number of
statements answered) = _ _ _ _ _ _
Average score for this section

Transfer your score to the
Telecommunications Analysis Index at
the beginning of the Self-Assessment.

# CRITERION #7: SUSTAIN:

INTENT: Retain the benefits.

In my belief, the answer to this
question is clearly defined:

5 Strongly Agree

4 Agree

3 Neutral

2 Disagree

1 Strongly Disagree

1. Is your strategy driving your strategy? Or is the way
in which you allocate resources driving your strategy?
<--- Score

2. How do you assess the Telecommunications
Analysis pitfalls that are inherent in implementing it?
<--- Score

**3. What is the big Telecommunications Analysis
idea?**
<--- Score

4. If you got fired and a new hire took your place, what would she do different?
<--- Score

**5. Who uses your product in ways you never expected?**
<--- Score

6. What potential megatrends could make your business model obsolete?
<--- Score

7. What knowledge, skills and characteristics mark a good Telecommunications Analysis project manager?
<--- Score

**8. Political -is anyone trying to undermine this project?**
<--- Score

9. What is an unauthorized commitment?
<--- Score

10. Will it be accepted by users?
<--- Score

11. How do customers see your organization?
<--- Score

**12. How do you make it meaningful in connecting Telecommunications Analysis with what users do day-to-day?**
<--- Score

13. How much does Telecommunications Analysis

help?

<--- Score

14. Do you say no to customers for no reason?

<--- Score

15. What stupid rule would you most like to kill?

<--- Score

16. How will you ensure you get what you expected?

<--- Score

**17. At what moment would you think; Will I get fired?**

<--- Score

18. What happens when a new employee joins the organization?

<--- Score

**19. Do you have enough freaky customers in your portfolio pushing you to the limit day in and day out?**

<--- Score

20. What are the short and long-term Telecommunications Analysis goals?

<--- Score

21. What is it like to work for you?

<--- Score

**22. Which functions and people interact with the supplier and or customer?**

<--- Score

23. What you are going to do to affect the numbers?
<--- Score

**24. What are the barriers to increased Telecommunications Analysis production?**
<--- Score

25. How do you engage the workforce, in addition to satisfying them?
<--- Score

**26. What is your Telecommunications Analysis strategy?**
<--- Score

**27. What did you miss in the interview for the worst hire you ever made?**
<--- Score

28. Who is the main stakeholder, with ultimate responsibility for driving Telecommunications Analysis forward?
<--- Score

29. What is your BATNA (best alternative to a negotiated agreement)?
<--- Score

**30. Is it economical; do you have the time and money?**
<--- Score

31. How do you determine the key elements that affect Telecommunications Analysis workforce satisfaction, how are these elements determined for different workforce groups and segments?

<--- Score

32. Is the Telecommunications Analysis organization completing tasks effectively and efficiently?
<--- Score

33. What are the long-term Telecommunications Analysis goals?
<--- Score

**34. Are assumptions made in Telecommunications Analysis stated explicitly?**
<--- Score

**35. If you had to rebuild your organization without any traditional competitive advantages (i.e., no killer technology, promising research, innovative product/service delivery model, etcetera), how would your people have to approach their work and collaborate together in order to create the necessary conditions for success?**
<--- Score

36. How will you insure seamless interoperability of Telecommunications Analysis moving forward?
<--- Score

37. How important is Telecommunications Analysis to the user organizations mission?
<--- Score

**38. Do you have past Telecommunications Analysis successes?**
<--- Score

**39. What management system can you use to**

**leverage the Telecommunications Analysis experience, ideas, and concerns of the people closest to the work to be done?**

<--- Score

40. How do you deal with Telecommunications Analysis changes?

<--- Score

41. What are the top 3 things at the forefront of your Telecommunications Analysis agendas for the next 3 years?

<--- Score

42. What is the range of capabilities?

<--- Score

**43. What is the source of the strategies for Telecommunications Analysis strengthening and reform?**

<--- Score

**44. In the past year, what have you done (or could you have done) to increase the accurate perception of your company/brand as ethical and honest?**

<--- Score

**45. What are the potential basics of Telecommunications Analysis fraud?**

<--- Score

**46. What new services of functionality will be implemented next with Telecommunications Analysis ?**

<--- Score

47. What are you trying to prove to yourself, and how might it be hijacking your life and business success?
<--- Score

**48. How do you lead with Telecommunications Analysis in mind?**
<--- Score

49. What is a feasible sequencing of reform initiatives over time?
<--- Score

50. What are the gaps in your knowledge and experience?
<--- Score

51. What are the usability implications of Telecommunications Analysis actions?
<--- Score

52. Are the criteria for selecting recommendations stated?
<--- Score

**53. Why not do Telecommunications Analysis?**
<--- Score

54. How do you stay inspired?
<--- Score

55. How do you foster innovation?
<--- Score

56. Do you see more potential in people than they do in themselves?

<--- Score

57. Do you think you know, or do you know you know
?
<--- Score

**58. How can you become the company that would put you out of business?**
<--- Score

**59. Who will provide the final approval of Telecommunications Analysis deliverables?**
<--- Score

60. Who have you, as a company, historically been when you've been at your best?
<--- Score

61. What could happen if you do not do it?
<--- Score

62. If there were zero limitations, what would you do differently?
<--- Score

63. What is the craziest thing you can do?
<--- Score

64. Is your basic point _____ or _____?
<--- Score

**65. Why do and why don't your customers like your organization?**
<--- Score

66. Marketing budgets are tighter, consumers are

more skeptical, and social media has changed forever the way we talk about Telecommunications Analysis, how do you gain traction?
<--- Score

67. Who is on the team?
<--- Score

68. How do you govern and fulfill your societal responsibilities?
<--- Score

69. What is something you believe that nearly no one agrees with you on?
<--- Score

70. What goals did you miss?
<--- Score

**71. What are specific Telecommunications Analysis rules to follow?**
<--- Score

72. What is your formula for success in Telecommunications Analysis ?
<--- Score

**73. If you weren't already in this business, would you enter it today? And if not, what are you going to do about it?**
<--- Score

74. Who is responsible for errors?
<--- Score

75. Which models, tools and techniques are

necessary?

<--- Score

76. What are the key enablers to make this Telecommunications Analysis move?

<--- Score

77. Who are your customers?

<--- Score

78. Can you do all this work?

<--- Score

**79. How do you foster the skills, knowledge, talents, attributes, and characteristics you want to have?**

<--- Score

**80. How do senior leaders deploy your organizations vision and values through your leadership system, to the workforce, to key suppliers and partners, and to customers and other stakeholders, as appropriate?**

<--- Score

81. How do you track customer value, profitability or financial return, organizational success, and sustainability?

<--- Score

82. How are you doing compared to your industry?

<--- Score

83. Is maximizing Telecommunications Analysis protection the same as minimizing Telecommunications Analysis loss?

<--- Score

84. Do Telecommunications Analysis rules make a reasonable demand on a users capabilities?
<--- Score

85. What happens at your organization when people fail?
<--- Score

86. Are the assumptions believable and achievable?
<--- Score

87. How do you manage Telecommunications Analysis Knowledge Management (KM)?
<--- Score

88. What is the kind of project structure that would be appropriate for your Telecommunications Analysis project, should it be formal and complex, or can it be less formal and relatively simple?
<--- Score

89. How do you keep records, of what?
<--- Score

**90. Who else should you help?**
<--- Score

**91. Which individuals, teams or departments will be involved in Telecommunications Analysis?**
<--- Score

**92. Who is responsible for Telecommunications Analysis?**
<--- Score

93. Are your responses positive or negative?
<--- Score

94. What Telecommunications Analysis modifications can you make work for you?
<--- Score

**95. Who, on the executive team or the board, has spoken to a customer recently?**
<--- Score

**96. How do you accomplish your long range Telecommunications Analysis goals?**
<--- Score

**97. How do you maintain Telecommunications Analysis's Integrity?**
<--- Score

98. What threat is Telecommunications Analysis addressing?
<--- Score

99. If you had to leave your organization for a year and the only communication you could have with employees/colleagues was a single paragraph, what would you write?
<--- Score

**100. Are you using a design thinking approach and integrating Innovation, Telecommunications Analysis Experience, and Brand Value?**
<--- Score

101. If you were responsible for initiating and

implementing major changes in your organization, what steps might you take to ensure acceptance of those changes?
<--- Score

102. How do you cross-sell and up-sell your Telecommunications Analysis success?
<--- Score

103. How do you set Telecommunications Analysis stretch targets and how do you get people to not only participate in setting these stretch targets but also that they strive to achieve these?
<--- Score

104. Are all key stakeholders present at all Structured Walkthroughs?
<--- Score

105. Why should people listen to you?
<--- Score

106. Did your employees make progress today?
<--- Score

107. What are the essentials of internal Telecommunications Analysis management?
<--- Score

108. Are you maintaining a past–present–future perspective throughout the Telecommunications Analysis discussion?
<--- Score

109. What are you challenging?
<--- Score

110. What was the last experiment you ran?
<--- Score

111. If your customer were your grandmother, would you tell her to buy what you're selling?
<--- Score

112. Whose voice (department, ethnic group, women, older workers, etc) might you have missed hearing from in your company, and how might you amplify this voice to create positive momentum for your business?
<--- Score

113. Do you know what you are doing? And who do you call if you don't?
<--- Score

114. What is the purpose of Telecommunications Analysis in relation to the mission?
<--- Score

115. What counts that you are not counting?
<--- Score

**116. What unique value proposition (UVP) do you offer?**
<--- Score

117. Has implementation been effective in reaching specified objectives so far?
<--- Score

118. How is implementation research currently incorporated into each of your goals?

<--- Score

119. What role does communication play in the success or failure of a Telecommunications Analysis project?
<--- Score

120. When information truly is ubiquitous, when reach and connectivity are completely global, when computing resources are infinite, and when a whole new set of impossibilities are not only possible, but happening, what will that do to your business?
<--- Score

**121. What trouble can you get into?**
<--- Score

122. If you do not follow, then how to lead?
<--- Score

123. To whom do you add value?
<--- Score

**124. What will be the consequences to the stakeholder (financial, reputation etc) if Telecommunications Analysis does not go ahead or fails to deliver the objectives?**
<--- Score

125. What must you excel at?
<--- Score

**126. How do you listen to customers to obtain actionable information?**
<--- Score

**127. What are strategies for increasing support and reducing opposition?**
<--- Score

128. What are your most important goals for the strategic Telecommunications Analysis objectives?
<--- Score

129. How can you incorporate support to ensure safe and effective use of Telecommunications Analysis into the services that you provide?
<--- Score

**130. Operational - will it work?**
<--- Score

**131. Do you have the right capabilities and capacities?**
<--- Score

**132. What is your competitive advantage?**
<--- Score

133. Would you rather sell to knowledgeable and informed customers or to uninformed customers?
<--- Score

134. What are current Telecommunications Analysis paradigms?
<--- Score

135. What is the estimated value of the project?
<--- Score

136. How will you motivate the stakeholders with the least vested interest?

<--- Score

137. What are your personal philosophies regarding Telecommunications Analysis and how do they influence your work?
<--- Score

**138. Are you / should you be revolutionary or evolutionary?**
<--- Score

139. Who will manage the integration of tools?
<--- Score

140. What would you recommend your friend do if he/she were facing this dilemma?
<--- Score

141. What have you done to protect your business from competitive encroachment?
<--- Score

142. If no one would ever find out about your accomplishments, how would you lead differently?
<--- Score

143. Who are four people whose careers you have enhanced?
<--- Score

**144. Is Telecommunications Analysis dependent on the successful delivery of a current project?**
<--- Score

145. Think of your Telecommunications Analysis project, what are the main functions?

<--- Score

146. Is there a work around that you can use?
<--- Score

147. What relationships among Telecommunications Analysis trends do you perceive?
<--- Score

148. Is Telecommunications Analysis realistic, or are you setting yourself up for failure?
<--- Score

149. How can you become more high-tech but still be high touch?
<--- Score

150. Where can you break convention?
<--- Score

**151. What would have to be true for the option on the table to be the best possible choice?**
<--- Score

152. What current systems have to be understood and/or changed?
<--- Score

**153. Can you maintain your growth without detracting from the factors that have contributed to your success?**
<--- Score

**154. How do you go about securing Telecommunications Analysis?**
<--- Score

155. Why is it important to have senior management support for a Telecommunications Analysis project?
<--- Score

156. What one word do you want to own in the minds of your customers, employees, and partners?
<--- Score

**157. How do you create buy-in?**
<--- Score

158. Do you have an implicit bias for capital investments over people investments?
<--- Score

159. What is the overall talent health of your organization as a whole at senior levels, and for each organization reporting to a member of the Senior Leadership Team?
<--- Score

**160. What information is critical to your organization that your executives are ignoring?**
<--- Score

161. How long will it take to change?
<--- Score

**162. What business benefits will Telecommunications Analysis goals deliver if achieved?**
<--- Score

163. Can the schedule be done in the given time?
<--- Score

164. What are the success criteria that will indicate that Telecommunications Analysis objectives have been met and the benefits delivered?

<--- Score

165. Do you feel that more should be done in the Telecommunications Analysis area?

<--- Score

166. Is there any existing Telecommunications Analysis governance structure?

<--- Score

167. What are the business goals Telecommunications Analysis is aiming to achieve?

<--- Score

168. Are you paying enough attention to the partners your company depends on to succeed?

<--- Score

169. How do you transition from the baseline to the target?

<--- Score

170. How do you ensure that implementations of Telecommunications Analysis products are done in a way that ensures safety?

<--- Score

171. What are the rules and assumptions your industry operates under? What if the opposite were true?

<--- Score

172. What does your signature ensure?

<--- Score

173. Why will customers want to buy your
organizations products/services?
<--- Score

**174. Will there be any necessary staff changes
(redundancies or new hires)?**
<--- Score

175. What is the funding source for this project?
<--- Score

**176. Who do we want your customers to become?**
<--- Score

177. What happens if you do not have enough
funding?
<--- Score

178. What are the performance and scale of the
Telecommunications Analysis tools?
<--- Score

179. Who are the key stakeholders?
<--- Score

180. Whom among your colleagues do you trust, and
for what?
<--- Score

181. What is your question? Why?
<--- Score

182. What have been your experiences in defining
long range Telecommunications Analysis goals?

<--- Score

183. Why should you adopt a Telecommunications Analysis framework?
<--- Score

184. Who will be responsible for deciding whether Telecommunications Analysis goes ahead or not after the initial investigations?
<--- Score

**185. How do you know if you are successful?**
<--- Score

186. Which Telecommunications Analysis goals are the most important?
<--- Score

187. How much contingency will be available in the budget?
<--- Score

188. Are there any activities that you can take off your to do list?
<--- Score

189. What is the recommended frequency of auditing?
<--- Score

190. Do you have the right people on the bus?
<--- Score

191. Ask yourself: how would you do this work if you only had one staff member to do it?
<--- Score

**192. How likely is it that a customer would recommend your company to a friend or colleague?**

<--- Score

**193. Why is Telecommunications Analysis important for you now?**

<--- Score

194. Is a Telecommunications Analysis team work effort in place?

<--- Score

195. How can you negotiate Telecommunications Analysis successfully with a stubborn boss, an irate client, or a deceitful coworker?

<--- Score

196. Are you making progress, and are you making progress as Telecommunications Analysis leaders?

<--- Score

197. What are internal and external Telecommunications Analysis relations?

<--- Score

198. If your company went out of business tomorrow, would anyone who doesn't get a paycheck here care?

<--- Score

199. If you find that you havent accomplished one of the goals for one of the steps of the Telecommunications Analysis strategy, what will you do to fix it?

<--- Score

200. What should you stop doing?
<--- Score

201. What are the challenges?
<--- Score

202. What Telecommunications Analysis skills are most important?
<--- Score

**203. How do you proactively clarify deliverables and Telecommunications Analysis quality expectations?**
<--- Score

204. How do you provide a safe environment -physically and emotionally?
<--- Score

**205. Can you break it down?**
<--- Score

206. Who do you think the world wants your organization to be?
<--- Score

207. Who is responsible for ensuring appropriate resources (time, people and money) are allocated to Telecommunications Analysis?
<--- Score

208. Is there any reason to believe the opposite of my current belief?
<--- Score

**209. Instead of going to current contacts for new**

**ideas, what if you reconnected with dormant contacts--the people you used to know?  If you were going reactivate a dormant tie, who would it be?**
<--- Score

210. Who will determine interim and final deadlines?
<--- Score

Add up total points for this section:
_ _ _ _ _ = Total points for this section

Divided by: _ _ _ _ _ _ (number of statements answered) = _ _ _ _ _ _
Average score for this section

Transfer your score to the Telecommunications Analysis Index at the beginning of the Self-Assessment.

# Telecommunications Analysis and Managing Projects, Criteria for Project Managers:

# 1.0 Initiating Process Group: Telecommunications Analysis

1. Who are the Telecommunications Analysis project stakeholders?

2. What are the short and long term implications?

3. Do you know the roles & responsibilities required for this Telecommunications Analysis project?

4. Who is involved in each phase?

5. Realistic - are the desired results expressed in a way that the team will be motivated and believe that the required level of involvement will be obtained?

6. When are the deliverables to be generated in each phase?

7. What must be done?

8. Who does what?

9. What business situation is being addressed?

10. Are you certain deliverables are properly completed and meet quality standards?

11. How do you help others satisfy needs?

12. During which stage of Risk planning are risks prioritized based on probability and impact?

13. Are the Telecommunications Analysis project

team and stakeholders meeting regularly and using a meeting agenda and taking notes to accurately document what is being covered and what happened in the weekly meetings?

14. How is each deliverable reviewed, verified, and validated?

15. At which stage, in a typical Telecommunications Analysis project do stake holders have maximum influence?

16. Have the stakeholders identified all individual requirements pertaining to business process?

17. Who is behind the Telecommunications Analysis project?

18. What were things that you did very well and want to do the same again on the next Telecommunications Analysis project?

19. What were things that you need to improve?

20. Will the Telecommunications Analysis project meet the client requirements, and will it achieve the business success criteria that justified doing the Telecommunications Analysis project in the first place?

# 1.1 Project Charter: Telecommunications Analysis

21. What are the constraints?

22. Why do you need to manage scope?

23. Does the Telecommunications Analysis project need to consider any special capacity or capability issues?

24. Why executive support?

25. Who manages integration?

26. Review the general mission What system will be affected by the improvement efforts?

27. What are the deliverables?

28. Who is the Telecommunications Analysis project Manager?

29. How will you know a change is an improvement?

30. When?

31. Dependent Telecommunications Analysis projects: what Telecommunications Analysis projects must be underway or completed before this Telecommunications Analysis project can be successful?

32. Who ise input and support will this Telecommunications Analysis project require?

33. Run it as as a startup?

34. What is in it for you?

35. Name and describe the elements that deal with providing the detail?

36. How much?

37. Is it an improvement over existing products?

38. When do you use a Telecommunications Analysis project Charter?

39. Why have you chosen the aim you have set forth?

40. If finished, on what date did it finish?

# 1.2 Stakeholder Register: Telecommunications Analysis

41. What & Why?

42. How should employers make voices heard?

43. What is the power of the stakeholder?

44. What opportunities exist to provide communications?

45. Who is managing stakeholder engagement?

46. Is your organization ready for change?

47. How much influence do they have on the Telecommunications Analysis project?

48. Who are the stakeholders?

49. What are the major Telecommunications Analysis project milestones requiring communications or providing communications opportunities?

50. How will reports be created?

51. How big is the gap?

52. Who wants to talk about Security?

# 1.3 Stakeholder Analysis Matrix: Telecommunications Analysis

53. Partnership opportunities/synergies?

54. What do you need to appraise?

55. Accreditations, qualifications, certifications?

56. New USPs?

57. How to measure the achievement of the Outputs?

58. Supporters; who are the supporters?

59. If the baseline is now, and if its improved it will be better than now?

60. Why do you need to manage Telecommunications Analysis project Risk?

61. How do customers express needs?

62. Volumes, production, economies?

63. What tools would help you communicate?

64. Who is most dependent on the resources at stake?

65. Continuity, supply chain robustness?

66. Which conditions out of the control of the management are crucial to contribute for the

achievement of the development objective?

67. Does your organization have bad debt or cash-flow problems?

68. How will the Telecommunications Analysis project benefit them?

69. Reputation, presence and reach?

70. What do you Evaluate?

71. Philosophy and values?

## 2.0 Planning Process Group: Telecommunications Analysis

72. Is the identification of the problems, inequalities and gaps, with respective causes, clear in the Telecommunications Analysis project?

73. Professionals want to know what is expected from them; what are the deliverables?

74. What good practices or successful experiences or transferable examples have been identified?

75. How should needs be met?

76. In which Telecommunications Analysis project management process group is the detailed Telecommunications Analysis project budget created?

77. How will you know you did it?

78. Mitigate. what will you do to minimize the impact should a risk event occur?

79. How are the principles of aid effectiveness (ownership, alignment, management for development results and mutual responsibility) being applied in the Telecommunications Analysis project?

80. To what extent is the program helping to influence your organizations policy framework?

81. When will the Telecommunications Analysis

project be done?

82. Are there efficient coordination mechanisms to avoid overloading the counterparts, participating stakeholders?

83. To what extent have public/private national resources and/or counterparts been mobilized to contribute to the programs objective and produce results and impacts?

84. What are the different approaches to building the WBS?

85. To what extent has the intervention strategy been adapted to the areas of intervention in which it is being implemented?

86. To what extent and in what ways are the Telecommunications Analysis project contributing to progress towards organizational reform?

87. How well do the team follow the chosen processes?

88. Telecommunications Analysis project assessment; why did you do this Telecommunications Analysis project?

89. Are you just doing busywork to pass the time?

90. Will the products created live up to the necessary quality?

91. The Telecommunications Analysis project charter is created in which Telecommunications Analysis

project management process group?

# 2.1 Project Management Plan: Telecommunications Analysis

92. Are comparable cost estimates used for comparing, screening and selecting alternative plans, and has a reasonable cost estimate been developed for the recommended plan?

93. Are alternatives safe, functional, constructible, economical, reasonable and sustainable?

94. How do you manage time?

95. What went wrong?

96. What happened during the process that you found interesting?

97. Who is the sponsor?

98. What data/reports/tools/etc. do your PMs need?

99. Is the appropriate plan selected based on your organizations objectives and evaluation criteria expressed in Principles and Guidelines policies?

100. How well are you able to manage your risk?

101. Are there any client staffing expectations?

102. What are the training needs?

103. Is mitigation authorized or recommended?

104. Are calculations and results of analyzes essentially correct?

105. Is the engineering content at a feasibility level-of-detail, and is it sufficiently complete, to provide an adequate basis for the baseline cost estimate?

106. Development trends and opportunities. What if the positive direction and vision of your organization causes expected trends to change?

107. Why Change?

108. What is the business need?

109. What is the justification?

110. Does the implementation plan have an appropriate division of responsibilities?

## 2.2 Scope Management Plan: Telecommunications Analysis

111. Is each item clearly and completely defined?

112. Can the Telecommunications Analysis project team do several activities in parallel?

113. Are the Telecommunications Analysis project team members located locally to the users/stakeholders?

114. Will the Telecommunications Analysis project deliverables become accepted in writing?

115. Has your organization done similar tasks before?

116. Has the budget been baselined?

117. What happens if scope changes?

118. Are Telecommunications Analysis project contact logs kept up to date?

119. How do you know how you are doing?

120. What happens to rejected deliverables?

121. Did your Telecommunications Analysis project ask for this?

122. Are there any scope changes proposed for the previously authorized Telecommunications Analysis

project?

123. Is there any form of automated support for Issues Management?

124. Has the selected plan been formulated using cost effectiveness and incremental analysis techniques?

125. Do you keep stake holders informed?

126. What weaknesses do you have?

127. Does the detailed work plan match the complexity of tasks with the capabilities of personnel?

128. Are risk triggers captured?

129. What should you drop in order to add something new?

# 2.3 Requirements Management Plan: Telecommunications Analysis

130. Will you document changes to requirements?

131. Will you have access to stakeholders when you need them?

132. Is there formal agreement on who has authority to approve a change in requirements?

133. Will you use tracing to help understand the impact of a change in requirements?

134. Are actual resource expenditures versus planned still acceptable?

135. Are actual resources expenditures versus planned expenditures acceptable?

136. What information regarding the Telecommunications Analysis project requirements will be reported?

137. Define the help desk model. who will take full responsibility?

138. Who has the authority to reject Telecommunications Analysis project requirements?

139. Should you include sub-activities?

140. Have stakeholders been instructed in the Change

Control process?

141. Did you provide clear and concise specifications?

142. How often will the reporting occur?

143. Is any organizational data being used or stored?

144. How knowledgeable is the primary Stakeholder(s) in the proposed application area?

145. Did you avoid subjective, flowery or non-specific statements?

146. Do you know which stakeholders will participate in the requirements effort?

147. How will the requirements become prioritized?

148. Who is responsible for quantifying the Telecommunications Analysis project requirements?

149. Which hardware or software, related to, or as outcome of the Telecommunications Analysis project is new to your organization?

# 2.4 Requirements Documentation: Telecommunications Analysis

150. How to document system requirements?

151. Can you check system requirements?

152. How will requirements be documented and who signs off on them?

153. Does your organization restrict technical alternatives?

154. Is new technology needed?

155. If applicable; are there issues linked with the fact that this is an offshore Telecommunications Analysis project?

156. Can the requirements be checked?

157. What will be the integration problems?

158. Who is interacting with the system?

159. How can you document system requirements?

160. What variations exist for a process?

161. Are all functions required by the customer included?

162. How much does requirements engineering cost?

163. Verifiability. can the requirements be checked?

164. What marketing channels do you want to use: e-mail, letter or sms?

165. How linear / iterative is your Requirements Gathering process (or will it be)?

166. Where are business rules being captured?

167. Who provides requirements?

168. What happens when requirements are wrong?

169. How will they be documented / shared?

## 2.5 Requirements Traceability Matrix: Telecommunications Analysis

170. What percentage of Telecommunications Analysis projects are producing traceability matrices between requirements and other work products?

171. What is the WBS?

172. Why do you manage scope?

173. Describe the process for approving requirements so they can be added to the traceability matrix and Telecommunications Analysis project work can be performed. Will the Telecommunications Analysis project requirements become approved in writing?

174. How will it affect the stakeholders personally in career?

175. What are the chronologies, contingencies, consequences, criteria?

176. Will you use a Requirements Traceability Matrix?

177. How do you manage scope?

178. How small is small enough?

179. Is there a requirements traceability process in place?

180. Do you have a clear understanding of all

subcontracts in place?

**181. Why use a WBS?**

# 2.6 Project Scope Statement: Telecommunications Analysis

182. Is the plan for Telecommunications Analysis project resources adequate?

183. Relevant - ask yourself can you get there; why are you doing this Telecommunications Analysis project?

184. Will the risk plan be updated on a regular and frequent basis?

185. How will you verify the accuracy of the work of the Telecommunications Analysis project, and what constitutes acceptance of the deliverables?

186. Do you anticipate new stakeholders joining the Telecommunications Analysis project over time?

187. Is the plan for your organization of the Telecommunications Analysis project resources adequate?

188. What actions will be taken to mitigate the risk?

189. Will tasks be marked complete only after QA has been successfully completed?

190. Elements that deal with providing the detail?

191. Was planning completed before the Telecommunications Analysis project was initiated?

192. Are there completion/verification criteria defined for each task producing an output?

193. Is your organization structure appropriate for the Telecommunications Analysis projects size and complexity?

194. Elements of scope management that deal with concept development ?

195. What is change?

196. Will all tasks resulting from issues be entered into the Telecommunications Analysis project Plan and tracked through the plan?

197. Did your Telecommunications Analysis project ask for this?

198. Were key Telecommunications Analysis project stakeholders brought into the Telecommunications Analysis project Plan?

199. Is an issue management process documented and filed?

200. What is the most common tool for helping define the detail?

201. What went right?

# 2.7 Assumption and Constraint Log: Telecommunications Analysis

202. Is there documentation of system capability requirements, data requirements, environment requirements, security requirements, and computer and hardware requirements?

203. Has the approach and development strategy of the Telecommunications Analysis project been defined, documented and accepted by the appropriate stakeholders?

204. What strengths do you have?

205. What would you gain if you spent time working to improve this process?

206. Have adequate resources been provided by management to ensure Telecommunications Analysis project success?

207. Are there processes in place to ensure internal consistency between the source code components?

208. Can you perform this task or activity in a more effective manner?

209. Does the plan conform to standards?

210. Are there cosmetic errors that hinder readability and comprehension?

211. Do the requirements meet the standards of correctness, completeness, consistency, accuracy, and readability?

212. What threats might prevent you from getting there?

213. Are there processes defining how software will be developed including development methods, overall timeline for development, software product standards, and traceability?

214. Are there processes in place to ensure that all the terms and code concepts have been documented consistently?

215. Is the definition of the Telecommunications Analysis project scope clear; what needs to be accomplished?

216. Has a Telecommunications Analysis project Communications Plan been developed?

217. What is positive about the current process?

218. Are there ways to reduce the time it takes to get something approved?

219. Are there standards for code development?

220. Is this model reasonable?

# 2.8 Work Breakdown Structure: Telecommunications Analysis

221. When do you stop?

222. How will you and your Telecommunications Analysis project team define the Telecommunications Analysis projects scope and work breakdown structure?

223. Why is it useful?

224. When does it have to be done?

225. What is the probability of completing the Telecommunications Analysis project in less that xx days?

226. Can you make it?

227. Is the work breakdown structure (wbs) defined and is the scope of the Telecommunications Analysis project clear with assigned deliverable owners?

228. Is it a change in scope?

229. When would you develop a Work Breakdown Structure?

230. Where does it take place?

231. How big is a work-package?

232. Who has to do it?

233. How many levels?

234. What is the probability that the Telecommunications Analysis project duration will exceed xx weeks?

235. What has to be done?

236. How much detail?

237. How far down?

# 2.9 WBS Dictionary: Telecommunications Analysis

238. Are indirect costs accumulated for comparison with the corresponding budgets?

239. Are management actions taken to reduce indirect costs when there are significant adverse variances?

240. Software specification, development, integration, and testing, licenses ?

241. What size should a work package be?

242. What is wrong with this Telecommunications Analysis project?

243. All cwbs elements specified for external reporting?

244. Are estimates developed by Telecommunications Analysis project personnel coordinated with the already stated responsible for overall management to determine whether required resources will be available according to revised planning?

245. Major functional areas of contract effort?

246. The Telecommunications Analysis projected business base for each period?

247. The already stated responsible for overhead

performance control of related costs?

248. Intermediate schedules, as required, which provide a logical sequence from the master schedule to the control account level?

249. Is the anticipated (firm and potential) business base Telecommunications Analysis projected in a rational, consistent manner?

250. Is each control account assigned to a single organizational element directly responsible for the work and identifiable to a single element of the CWBS?

251. Are work packages assigned to performing organizations?

252. What are you counting on?

253. Are the bases and rates for allocating costs from each indirect pool to commercial work consistent with the already stated used to allocate corresponding costs to Government contracts?

254. Budgets assigned to control accounts?

255. Are all elements of indirect expense identified to overhead cost budgets of Telecommunications Analysis projections?

256. Evaluate the performance of operating organizations?

257. Do the lines of authority for incurring indirect costs correspond to the lines of responsibility for

management control of the same components of
costs?

# 2.10 Schedule Management Plan: Telecommunications Analysis

258. Is there a formal process for updating the Telecommunications Analysis project baseline?

259. Is the steering committee active in Telecommunications Analysis project oversight?

260. What is the difference between % Complete and % work?

261. Are the Telecommunications Analysis project team members located locally to the users/stakeholders?

262. Are Telecommunications Analysis project team members committed fulltime?

263. Are action items captured and managed?

264. Is it standard practice to formally commit stakeholders to the Telecommunications Analysis project via agreements?

265. Will rolling way planning be used?

266. Are the predecessor and successor relationships accurate?

267. How does the proposed individual meet each requirement?

268. Is current scope of the Telecommunications Analysis project substantially different than that originally defined?

269. Are the people assigned to the Telecommunications Analysis project sufficiently qualified?

270. Have all team members been part of identifying risks?

271. What does a valid Schedule look like?

272. Are metrics used to evaluate and manage Vendors?

273. Has a resource management plan been created?

274. Are all payments made according to the contract(s)?

275. Are cause and effect determined for risks when they occur?

276. Is a process for scheduling and reporting defined, including forms and formats?

277. Are the payment terms being followed?

# 2.11 Activity List: Telecommunications Analysis

278. How difficult will it be to do specific activities on this Telecommunications Analysis project?

279. How detailed should a Telecommunications Analysis project get?

280. What is the probability the Telecommunications Analysis project can be completed in xx weeks?

281. What is the LF and LS for each activity?

282. How will it be performed?

283. How should ongoing costs be monitored to try to keep the Telecommunications Analysis project within budget?

284. When will the work be performed?

285. How can the Telecommunications Analysis project be displayed graphically to better visualize the activities?

286. Who will perform the work?

287. What are the critical bottleneck activities?

288. How much slack is available in the Telecommunications Analysis project?

289. Where will it be performed?

290. When do the individual activities need to start and finish?

291. How do you determine the late start (LS) for each activity?

292. What is your organizations history in doing similar activities?

293. Are the required resources available or need to be acquired?

294. Can you determine the activity that must finish, before this activity can start?

295. The wbs is developed as part of a joint planning session. and how do you know that youhave done this right?

## 2.12 Activity Attributes: Telecommunications Analysis

296. How else could the items be grouped?

297. How many resources do you need to complete the work scope within a limit of X number of days?

298. Which method produces the more accurate cost assignment?

299. Activity: fair or not fair?

300. Resource is assigned to?

301. Does your organization of the data change its meaning?

302. Where else does it apply?

303. Do you feel very comfortable with your prediction?

304. Time for overtime?

305. Resources to accomplish the work?

306. Would you consider either of corresponding activities an outlier?

307. Activity: what is In the Bag?

308. How difficult will it be to complete specific

activities on this Telecommunications Analysis project?

309. Why?

310. How difficult will it be to do specific activities on this Telecommunications Analysis project?

311. What activity do you think you should spend the most time on?

312. Can more resources be added?

313. What conclusions/generalizations can you draw from this?

# 2.13 Milestone List: Telecommunications Analysis

314. How late can the activity finish?

315. When will the Telecommunications Analysis project be complete?

316. Information and research?

317. How late can the activity start?

318. Describe the industry you are in and the market growth opportunities. What is the market for your technology, product or service?

319. Do you foresee any technical risks or developmental challenges?

320. Vital contracts and partners?

321. Can you derive how soon can the whole Telecommunications Analysis project finish?

322. How soon can the activity start?

323. Describe your organizations strengths and core competencies. What factors will make your organization succeed?

324. Sustainable financial backing?

325. Describe the concept of the technology, product

or service that will be or has been developed. How will it be used?

326. Marketing - reach, distribution, awareness?

327. How difficult will it be to do specific activities on this Telecommunications Analysis project?

328. What is the market for your technology, product or service?

329. Timescales, deadlines and pressures?

330. Usps (unique selling points)?

331. What specific improvements did you make to the Telecommunications Analysis project proposal since the previous time?

# 2.14 Network Diagram: Telecommunications Analysis

332. What are the Key Success Factors?

333. What can be done concurrently?

334. If the Telecommunications Analysis project network diagram cannot change and you have extra personnel resources, what is the BEST thing to do?

335. Which type of network diagram allows you to depict four types of dependencies?

336. Where do schedules come from?

337. Exercise: what is the probability that the Telecommunications Analysis project duration will exceed xx weeks?

338. Are the gantt chart and/or network diagram updated periodically and used to assess the overall Telecommunications Analysis project timetable?

339. What is the probability of completing the Telecommunications Analysis project in less that xx days?

340. What activity must be completed immediately before this activity can start?

341. How difficult will it be to do specific activities on this Telecommunications Analysis project?

342. What to do and When?

343. Review the logical flow of the network diagram. Take a look at which activities you have first and then sequence the activities. Do they make sense?

344. Why must you schedule milestones, such as reviews, throughout the Telecommunications Analysis project?

345. What controls the start and finish of a job?

346. What activities must follow this activity?

347. What are the tools?

348. What must be completed before an activity can be started?

349. Are you on time?

350. What is the lowest cost to complete this Telecommunications Analysis project in xx weeks?

## 2.15 Activity Resource Requirements: Telecommunications Analysis

351. How many signatures do you require on a check and does this match what is in your policy and procedures?

352. When does monitoring begin?

353. Organizational Applicability?

354. Is there anything planned that does not need to be here?

355. Anything else?

356. Other support in specific areas?

357. Which logical relationship does the PDM use most often?

358. How do you handle petty cash?

359. What are constraints that you might find during the Human Resource Planning process?

360. Why do you do that?

361. Are there unresolved issues that need to be addressed?

362. What is the Work Plan Standard?

363. Do you use tools like decomposition and rolling-wave planning to produce the activity list and other outputs?

# 2.16 Resource Breakdown Structure: Telecommunications Analysis

364. Who needs what information?

365. Who is allowed to perform which functions?

366. What is the primary purpose of the human resource plan?

367. What defines a successful Telecommunications Analysis project?

368. What defines a successful Telecommunications Analysis project?

369. What is Telecommunications Analysis project communication management?

370. What is the purpose of assigning and documenting responsibility?

371. What can you do to improve productivity?

372. Who is allowed to see what data about which resources?

373. Who delivers the information?

374. What is the number one predictor of a groups productivity?

375. When do they need the information?

376. Why do you do it?

377. Any changes from stakeholders?

378. Why is this important?

379. Why time management?

# 2.17 Activity Duration Estimates: Telecommunications Analysis

380. What functions does this software provide that cannot be done easily using other tools such as a spreadsheet or database?

381. What are the main parts of a scope statement?

382. Which best describes how this affects the Telecommunications Analysis project?

383. Are adjustments implemented to correct or prevent defects?

384. What are key inputs and outputs of the software?

385. Why is there a new or renewed interest in the field of Telecommunications Analysis project management?

386. After changes are approved are Telecommunications Analysis project documents updated and distributed?

387. If the optimiztic estimate for an activity is 12days, and the pessimistic estimate is 18days, what is the standard deviation of this activity?

388. Which type of mathematical analysis is being used?

389. Explanation notice how many choices are half

right?

390. Does a process exist to formally recognize new Telecommunications Analysis projects?

391. What tasks must follow this task?

392. Why should Telecommunications Analysis project managers strive to make jobs look easy?

393. Does a process exist to identify which qualified resources may be attainable?

394. Are Telecommunications Analysis project results verified and Telecommunications Analysis project documents archived?

395. Account for the four frames of organizations. How can they help Telecommunications Analysis project managers understand your organizational context for Telecommunications Analysis projects?

396. Is evaluation criteria defined to rate proposals?

397. Did anything besides luck make a difference between success and failure?

## 2.18 Duration Estimating Worksheet: Telecommunications Analysis

398. What is next?

399. How can the Telecommunications Analysis project be displayed graphically to better visualize the activities?

400. Do any colleagues have experience with your organization and/or RFPs?

401. What questions do you have?

402. What info is needed?

403. Is this operation cost effective?

404. Small or large Telecommunications Analysis project?

405. Value pocket identification & quantification what are value pockets?

406. Can the Telecommunications Analysis project be constructed as planned?

407. Define the work as completely as possible. What work will be included in the Telecommunications Analysis project?

408. Is the Telecommunications Analysis project responsive to community need?

409. Science = process: remember the scientific method?

410. When, then?

411. What is your role?

412. How should ongoing costs be monitored to try to keep the Telecommunications Analysis project within budget?

413. What work will be included in the Telecommunications Analysis project?

414. Why estimate costs?

# 2.19 Project Schedule: Telecommunications Analysis

415. What is risk management?

416. Verify that the update is accurate. Are all remaining durations correct?

417. Why do you think schedule issues often cause the most conflicts on Telecommunications Analysis projects?

418. Are there activities that came from a template or previous Telecommunications Analysis project that are not applicable on this phase of this Telecommunications Analysis project?

419. Why or why not?

420. Are activities connected because logic dictates the order in which others occur?

421. Telecommunications Analysis project work estimates Who is managing the work estimate quality of work tasks in the Telecommunications Analysis project schedule?

422. What is the purpose of a Telecommunications Analysis project schedule?

423. How does a Telecommunications Analysis project get to be a year late ?

424. Your best shot for providing estimations how complex/how much work does the activity require?

425. Did the Telecommunications Analysis project come in under budget?

426. Are key risk mitigation strategies added to the Telecommunications Analysis project schedule?

427. If you can not fix it, how do you do it differently?

428. What is Telecommunications Analysis project management?

429. How can slack be negative?

430. How effectively were issues able to be resolved without impacting the Telecommunications Analysis project Schedule or Budget?

431. Schedule/cost recovery?

432. What is risk?

433. How do you know that youhave done this right?

## 2.20 Cost Management Plan: Telecommunications Analysis

434. What is cost and Telecommunications Analysis project cost management?

435. Pareto diagrams, statistical sampling, flow charting or trend analysis used quality monitoring?

436. Have all necessary approvals been obtained?

437. How difficult will it be to do specific tasks on the Telecommunications Analysis project?

438. Are meeting minutes captured and sent out after the meeting?

439. Weve met your goals?

440. Are any non-compliance issues that exist due to State practices communicated to your organization?

441. Has a structured approach been used to break work effort into manageable components (WBS)?

442. Is there a formal set of procedures supporting Stakeholder Management?

443. Do Telecommunications Analysis project teams & team members report on status / activities / progress?

444. Are trade-offs between accepting the risk and mitigating the risk identified?

445. Cost management – how will the cost of changes be estimated and controlled?

446. Is there an on-going process in place to monitor Telecommunications Analysis project risks?

447. Ranged estimates?

448. Does the Telecommunications Analysis project have a Quality Culture?

449. Are tasks tracked by hours?

450. Is there a formal process for updating the Telecommunications Analysis project baseline?

451. Forecasts – how will the time and resources needed to complete the Telecommunications Analysis project be forecast?

452. Telecommunications Analysis project definition & scope?

## 2.21 Activity Cost Estimates: Telecommunications Analysis

453. Certification of actual expenditures?

454. How do you manage cost?

455. Does the estimator have experience?

456. How do you change activities?

457. One way to define activities is to consider how organization employees describe jobs to families and friends. You basically want to know, What do you do?

458. Who & what determines the need for contracted services?

459. What makes a good activity description?

460. Were sponsors and decision makers available when needed outside regularly scheduled meetings?

461. Performance bond should always provide what part of the contract value?

462. What is the Telecommunications Analysis projects sustainability strategy that will ensure Telecommunications Analysis project results will endure or be sustained?

463. Where can you get activity reports?

464. Does the activity use a common approach or business function to deliver its results?

465. Which contract type places the most risk on the seller?

466. How do you fund change orders?

467. Were you satisfied with the work?

468. How quickly can the task be done with the skills available?

469. The impact and what actions were taken?

470. How do you allocate indirect costs to activities?

# 2.22 Cost Estimating Worksheet: Telecommunications Analysis

471. Identify the timeframe necessary to monitor progress and collect data to determine how the selected measure has changed?

472. Can a trend be established from historical performance data on the selected measure and are the criteria for using trend analysis or forecasting methods met?

473. Is the Telecommunications Analysis project responsive to community need?

474. What costs are to be estimated?

475. Will the Telecommunications Analysis project collaborate with the local community and leverage resources?

476. Is it feasible to establish a control group arrangement?

477. Ask: are others positioned to know, are others credible, and will others cooperate?

478. How will the results be shared and to whom?

479. What is the estimated labor cost today based upon this information?

480. What additional Telecommunications Analysis

project(s) could be initiated as a result of this Telecommunications Analysis project?

481. What can be included?

482. What will others want?

483. Who is best positioned to know and assist in identifying corresponding factors?

484. What is the purpose of estimating?

485. Does the Telecommunications Analysis project provide innovative ways for stakeholders to overcome obstacles or deliver better outcomes?

486. What happens to any remaining funds not used?

# 2.23 Cost Baseline: Telecommunications Analysis

487. Does a process exist for establishing a cost baseline to measure Telecommunications Analysis project performance?

488. Are procedures defined by which the cost baseline may be changed?

489. Has the appropriate access to relevant data and analysis capability been granted?

490. How accurate do cost estimates need to be?

491. Have all the product or service deliverables been accepted by the customer?

492. On time?

493. At which frequency ?

494. Is request in line with priorities?

495. Has the Telecommunications Analysis project documentation been archived or otherwise disposed as described in the Telecommunications Analysis project communication plan?

496. Does the suggested change request seem to represent a necessary enhancement to the product?

497. How difficult will it be to do specific tasks on the

Telecommunications Analysis project?

498. Have all approved changes to the schedule baseline been identified and impact on the Telecommunications Analysis project documented?

499. What is your organizations history in doing similar tasks?

500. Has the documentation relating to operation and maintenance of the product(s) or service(s) been delivered to, and accepted by, operations management?

501. Definition of done can be traced back to the definitions of what are you providing to the customer in terms of deliverables?

502. On budget?

503. Have the lessons learned been filed with the Telecommunications Analysis project Management Office?

504. What can go wrong?

505. For what purpose ?

506. How concrete were original objectives?

# 2.24 Quality Management Plan: Telecommunications Analysis

507. After observing execution of process, is it in compliance with the documented Plan?

508. How will you know that a change is actually an improvement?

509. What is the Quality Management Plan?

510. How does your organization ensure the reliability, accuracy, timeliness, security and accessibility of data and information?

511. Results Available?

512. What is the audience for the data?

513. What is the Difference Between a QMP and QAPP?

514. What other teams / processes would be impacted by changes to the current process, and how?

515. How does your organization decide what to measure?

516. How do you document and correct nonconformances?

517. How are records kept in the office?

518. When reporting to different audiences, do you vary the form or type of report?

519. Are there trends or hot spots?

520. How are people conducting sampling trained?

521. Who is responsible?

522. How do senior leaders review organizational performance?

523. How long do you retain data?

524. How does the material compare to a regulatory threshold?

## 2.25 Quality Metrics: Telecommunications Analysis

525. How are requirements conflicts resolved?

526. Do the operators focus on determining; is there anything you need to worry about?

527. What group is empowered to define quality requirements?

528. How do you know if everyone is trying to improve the right things?

529. What approved evidence based screening tools can be used?

530. Is there a set of procedures to capture, analyze and act on quality metrics?

531. What metrics do you measure?

532. What does this tell us?

533. Were quality attributes reported?

534. Filter visualizations of interest?

535. How exactly do you define when differences exist?

536. What level of statistical confidence do you use?

537. Do you know how much profit a 10% decrease in waste would generate?

538. Why is now the time for quality metrics?

539. What happens if you get an abnormal result?

540. What is the timeline to meet your goal?

541. Does risk analysis documentation meet standards?

542. How do you measure?

543. Where did complaints, returns and warranty claims come from?

544. Are applicable standards referenced and available?

## 2.26 Process Improvement Plan: Telecommunications Analysis

545. Does your process ensure quality?

546. What is the test-cycle concept?

547. Have storage and access mechanisms and procedures been determined?

548. What is the return on investment?

549. Who should prepare the process improvement action plan?

550. Where do you want to be?

551. Modeling current processes is great, and will you ever see a return on that investment?

552. Are you meeting the quality standards?

553. The motive is determined by asking, Why do you want to achieve this goal?

554. Are there forms and procedures to collect and record the data?

555. What makes people good SPI coaches?

556. What personnel are the change agents for your initiative?

557. Where are you now?

558. Where do you focus?

559. Are you making progress on the goals?

560. What personnel are the coaches for your initiative?

561. What is quality and how will you ensure it?

562. Have the supporting tools been developed or acquired?

563. Does explicit definition of the measures exist?

## 2.27 Responsibility Assignment Matrix: Telecommunications Analysis

564. Past experience – the person or the group worked at something similar in the past?

565. Identify potential or actual overruns and underruns?

566. Is work progressively subdivided into detailed work packages as requirements are defined?

567. Does the contractor use objective results, design reviews and tests to trace schedule performance?

568. Do managers and team members provide helpful suggestions during review meetings?

569. Are the wbs and organizational levels for application of the Telecommunications Analysis projected overhead costs identified?

570. The already stated responsible for the establishment of budgets and assignment of resources for overhead performance?

571. Availability – will the group or the person be available within the necessary time interval?

572. With too many people labeled as doing the work, are there too many hands involved?

573. Do all the identified groups or people really need

to be consulted?

574. Does the scheduling system identify in a timely manner the status of work?

575. Are your organizations and items of cost assigned to each pool identified?

576. Are overhead cost budgets established for each organization which has authority to incur overhead costs?

577. Is the anticipated (firm and potential) business base Telecommunications Analysis projected in a rational, consistent manner?

578. Undistributed budgets, if any?

579. What expertise is available in your department?

580. Most people let you know when others re too busy, and are others really too busy?

581. What simple tool can you use to help identify and prioritize Telecommunications Analysis project risks that is very low tech and high touch?

582. Is work properly classified as measured effort, LOE, or apportioned effort and appropriately separated?

# 2.28 Roles and Responsibilities: Telecommunications Analysis

583. Have you ever been a part of this team?

584. How is your work-life balance?

585. What should you do now to prepare yourself for a promotion, increased responsibilities or a different job?

586. What is working well?

587. Who is involved?

588. What should you do now to ensure that you are meeting all expectations of your current position?

589. What should you do now to prepare for your career 5+ years from now?

590. Is there a training program in place for stakeholders covering expectations, roles and responsibilities and any addition knowledge others need to be good stakeholders?

591. What expectations were met?

592. To decide whether to use a quality measurement, ask how will you know when it is achieved?

593. Does the team have access to and ability to use data analysis tools?

594. Is the data complete?

595. Once the responsibilities are defined for the Telecommunications Analysis project, have the deliverables, roles and responsibilities been clearly communicated to every participant?

596. What areas would you highlight for changes or improvements?

597. What is working well within your organizations performance management system?

598. What specific behaviors did you observe?

599. Was the expectation clearly communicated?

600. Implementation of actions: Who are the responsible units?

## 2.29 Human Resource Management Plan: Telecommunications Analysis

601. Is quality monitored from the perspective of the customers needs and expectations?

602. Are people motivated to meet the current and future challenges?

603. Quality assurance overheads?

604. Is this Telecommunications Analysis project carried out in partnership with other groups/ organizations?

605. Timeline and milestones?

606. Has the Telecommunications Analysis project scope been baselined?

607. Has the schedule been baselined?

608. Are estimating assumptions and constraints captured?

609. Do Telecommunications Analysis project managers participating in the Telecommunications Analysis project know the Telecommunications Analysis projects true status first hand?

610. How to convince to employees that it is a necessary process?

611. Does the Telecommunications Analysis project have a Quality Culture?

612. Have stakeholder accountabilities & responsibilities been clearly defined?

613. Is the communication plan being followed?

614. Are change requests logged and managed?

615. Is there an issues management plan in place?

616. What is this Telecommunications Analysis project aiming to achieve?

617. Do you have the reasons why the changes to your organizational systems and capabilities are required?

618. Are there dependencies with other initiatives or Telecommunications Analysis projects?

619. Are Telecommunications Analysis project team members involved in detailed estimating and scheduling?

# 2.30 Communications Management Plan: Telecommunications Analysis

620. Who to share with?

621. Timing: when do the effects of the communication take place?

622. Which team member will work with each stakeholder?

623. What data is going to be required?

624. What are the interrelationships?

625. Why is stakeholder engagement important?

626. How did the term stakeholder originate?

627. What is the political influence?

628. Is there an important stakeholder who is actively opposed and will not receive messages?

629. How will the person responsible for executing the communication item be notified?

630. What is Telecommunications Analysis project communications management?

631. Do you prepare stakeholder engagement plans?

632. What does the stakeholder need from the team?

633. What is the stakeholders level of authority?

634. What approaches do you use?

635. Who were proponents/opponents?

636. Do you feel a register helps?

637. Who have you worked with in past, similar initiatives?

638. Are the stakeholders getting the information others need, are others consulted, are concerns addressed?

# 2.31 Risk Management Plan: Telecommunications Analysis

639. Risk categories: what are the main categories of risks that should be addressed on this Telecommunications Analysis project?

640. Are tools for analysis and design available?

641. Is there anything you would now do differently on your Telecommunications Analysis project based on this experience?

642. What does a risk management program do?

643. Should the risk be taken at all?

644. What are the cost, schedule and resource impacts if the risk does occur?

645. Was an original risk assessment/risk management plan completed?

646. Management -what contingency plans do you have if the risk becomes a reality?

647. Do the requirements require the creation of components that are unlike anything your organization has previously built?

648. Is the customer willing to participate in reviews?

649. Risk probability and impact: how will the

probabilities and impacts of risk items be assessed?

650. Litigation – what is the probability that lawsuits will cause problems or delays in the Telecommunications Analysis project?

651. User involvement: do you have the right users?

652. Do you manage the process through use of metrics?

653. Market risk -will the new service or product be useful to your organization or marketable to others?

654. Are end-users enthusiastically committed to the Telecommunications Analysis project and the system/product to be built?

655. Why do you need to manage Telecommunications Analysis project Risk?

656. Are tool mentors available?

657. Do requirements put excessive performance constraints on the product?

658. What other risks are created by choosing an avoidance strategy?

# 2.32 Risk Register: Telecommunications Analysis

659. What is a Community Risk Register?

660. Schedule impact/severity estimated range (workdays) assume the event happens, what is the potential impact?

661. Are there any gaps in the evidence?

662. What can be done about it?

663. What are the main aims, objectives of the policy, strategy, or service and the intended outcomes?

664. Who is going to do it?

665. How could corresponding Risk affect the Telecommunications Analysis project in terms of cost and schedule?

666. Severity Prediction?

667. Do you require further engagement?

668. Have other controls and solutions been implemented in other services which could be applied as an alternative to additional funding?

669. What are you going to do to limit the Telecommunications Analysis projects risk exposure due to the identified risks?

670. How are risks graded?

671. Preventative actions - planned actions to reduce the likelihood a risk will occur and/or reduce the seriousness should it occur. What should you do now?

672. What should you do now?

673. Amongst the action plans and recommendations that you have to introduce are there some that could stop or delay the overall program?

674. What will be done?

675. Who is accountable?

676. Risk categories: what are the main categories of risks that should be addressed on this Telecommunications Analysis project?

677. Who needs to know about this?

# 2.33 Probability and Impact Assessment: Telecommunications Analysis

678. Can the risk be avoided by choosing a different alternative?

679. Your customers business requirements have suddenly shifted because of a new regulatory statute, what now?

680. My Telecommunications Analysis project leader has suddenly left your organization, what do you do?

681. How will the consumption pattern change?

682. What are the probabilities of chosen technologies being suitable for local conditions?

683. Do you use diagramming techniques to show cause and effect?

684. What risks does your organization have if the Telecommunications Analysis projects fail to meet deadline?

685. Is the process supported by tools?

686. What are the current or emerging trends of culture?

687. Do you use any methods to analyze risks?

688. Are some people working on multiple Telecommunications Analysis projects?

689. What are the chances the event will occur?

690. What will be the likely political situation during the life of the Telecommunications Analysis project?

691. How is the Telecommunications Analysis project going to be managed?

692. Is the present organizational structure for handling the Telecommunications Analysis project sufficient?

693. How would you suggest monitoring for risk transition indicators?

694. Are the facilities, expertise, resources, and management know-how available to handle the situation?

695. What is the risk appetite?

696. Risk may be made during which step of risk management?

697. Has the need for the Telecommunications Analysis project been properly established?

# 2.34 Probability and Impact Matrix: Telecommunications Analysis

698. What should be the gestation period for the Telecommunications Analysis project with this technology?

699. Has the need for the Telecommunications Analysis project been properly established?

700. Which of the risk factors can be avoided altogether?

701. Is the Telecommunications Analysis project cutting across the entire organization?

702. Are there alternative opinions/solutions/processes you should explore?

703. How would you assess the risk management process in the Telecommunications Analysis project?

704. Premium on reliability of product?

705. Maximize short-term return on investment?

706. Mandated delivery date?

707. What should be done with non-critical risks?

708. Do you know the order of planning yet?

709. What will the damage be?

710. How well is the risk understood?

711. Are you working on the right risks?

712. What are the ways you measure and evaluate risks?

713. What kind of preparation would be required to do this?

714. What can possibly go wrong?

715. Have top software and customer managers formally committed to support the Telecommunications Analysis project?

## 2.35 Risk Data Sheet: Telecommunications Analysis

716. What were the Causes that contributed?

717. Has a sensitivity analysis been carried out?

718. Type of risk identified?

719. What was measured?

720. What actions can be taken to eliminate or remove risk?

721. What will be the consequences if it happens?

722. How can it happen?

723. What are you weak at and therefore need to do better?

724. What do you know?

725. Has the most cost-effective solution been chosen?

726. What can happen?

727. Whom do you serve (customers)?

728. During work activities could hazards exist?

729. What are you trying to achieve (Objectives)?

730. What if client refuses?

731. What are you here for (Mission)?

732. What are the main opportunities available to you that you should grab while you can?

733. What is the likelihood of it happening?

## 2.36 Procurement Management Plan: Telecommunications Analysis

734. Are decisions made in a timely manner?

735. In which phase of the Acquisition Process Cycle does source qualifications reside?

736. Does the business case include how the Telecommunications Analysis project aligns with your organizations strategic goals & objectives?

737. Are decisions captured in a decisions log?

738. Specific - is the objective clear in terms of what, how, when, and where the situation will be changed?

739. Financial capacity; does the seller have, or can the seller reasonably be expected to obtain, the financial resources needed?

740. Has the business need been clearly defined?

741. Are quality inspections and review activities listed in the Telecommunications Analysis project schedule(s)?

742. Are the people assigned to the Telecommunications Analysis project sufficiently qualified?

743. How and when do you enter into Telecommunications Analysis project Procurement

Management?

744. Does all Telecommunications Analysis project documentation reside in a common repository for easy access?

745. Are status reports received per the Telecommunications Analysis project Plan?

746. Based on your Telecommunications Analysis project communication management plan, what worked well?

747. Do Telecommunications Analysis project managers participating in the Telecommunications Analysis project know the Telecommunications Analysis projects true status first hand?

748. What is a Telecommunications Analysis project Management Plan?

749. Have lessons learned been conducted after each Telecommunications Analysis project release?

# 2.37 Source Selection Criteria: Telecommunications Analysis

750. Are types/quantities of material, facilities appropriate?

751. How are clarifications and communications appropriately used?

752. What is the role of counsel in the procurement process?

753. What is the last item a Telecommunications Analysis project manager must do to finalize Telecommunications Analysis project close-out?

754. Are considerations anticipated?

755. If the costs are normalized, please account for how the normalization is conducted. Is a cost realism analysis used?

756. Can you make a cost/technical tradeoff?

757. Who must be notified?

758. What should be the contracting officers strategy?

759. What are the guiding principles for developing an evaluation report?

760. How organization are proposed quotes/prices?

761. What should be considered?

762. Can you prevent comparison of proposals?

763. How long will it take for the purchase cost to be the same as the lease cost?

764. What should clarifications include?

765. How can the methods of publicizing the buy be tailored to yield more effective price competition?

766. Why promote competition?

767. What should be considered when developing evaluation standards?

768. Can you reasonably estimate total organization requirements for the coming year?

769. Have team members been adequately trained?

# 2.38 Stakeholder Management Plan: Telecommunications Analysis

770. Are the schedule estimates reasonable given the Telecommunications Analysis project?

771. Who is gathering information?

772. Does the Telecommunications Analysis project have a Quality Culture?

773. Have key stakeholders been identified?

774. Are all vendor contracts closed out?

775. Does the system design reflect the requirements?

776. Are all key components of a Quality Assurance Plan present?

777. Are requirements management tracking tools and procedures in place?

778. Do all stakeholders know how to access this repository and where to find the Telecommunications Analysis project documentation?

779. Are meeting objectives identified for each meeting?

780. Has a capability assessment been conducted?

781. What has to be purchased?

782. Who will be responsible for managing and maintaining the Issues Register?

783. Has the Telecommunications Analysis project manager been identified?

784. What procedures will be utilised to ensure effective monitoring of Telecommunications Analysis project progress?

785. Are milestone deliverables effectively tracked and compared to Telecommunications Analysis project plan?

# 2.39 Change Management Plan: Telecommunications Analysis

786. How much change management is needed?

787. Will the readiness criteria be met prior to the training roll out?

788. What skills, education, knowledge, or work experiences should the resources have for each identified competency?

789. Who might present the most resistance?

790. How much Telecommunications Analysis project management is needed?

791. What is the negative impact of communicating too soon or too late?

792. Will a different work structure focus people on what is important?

793. Is a training information sheet available?

794. Has the training provider been established?

795. Who should be involved in developing a change management strategy?

796. What are the current methods of sharing information and do there need to be new ones developed?

797. Clearly articulate the overall business benefits of the Telecommunications Analysis project -why are you doing this now?

798. Has the relevant business unit been notified of installation and support requirements?

799. Have the systems been configured and tested?

800. Would you need to tailor a special message for each segment of the audience?

801. What are the key change management success metrics?

802. Do the proposed users have access to the appropriate documentation?

803. What risks may occur upfront?

804. What goal(s) do you hope to accomplish?

805. Different application of an existing process?

# 3.0 Executing Process Group: Telecommunications Analysis

806. How could stakeholders negatively impact your Telecommunications Analysis project?

807. What factors are contributing to progress or delay in the achievement of products and results?

808. Does software appear easy to learn?

809. Is the program supported by national and/or local organizations?

810. Will additional funds be needed for hardware or software?

811. What are the main types of goods and services being outsourced?

812. What type of people would you want on your team?

813. What is in place for ensuring adequate change control on Telecommunications Analysis projects that involve outside contracts?

814. Do schedule issues conflicts?

815. What Telecommunications Analysis projects and services are in the portfolio of your organization?

816. Are the necessary foundations in place to ensure

the sustainability of the results of the programme?

817. Could a new application negatively affect the current IT infrastructure?

818. How does a Telecommunications Analysis project life cycle differ from a product life cycle?

819. Does the case present a realistic scenario?

820. What are the Telecommunications Analysis project management deliverables of each process group?

821. After how many days will the lease cost be the same as the purchase cost for the equipment?

822. How well did the chosen processes produce the expected results?

823. What does it mean to take a systems view of a Telecommunications Analysis project?

824. What are the critical steps involved in selecting measures and initiatives?

825. Does the Telecommunications Analysis project team have enough people to execute the Telecommunications Analysis project plan?

# 3.1 Team Member Status Report: Telecommunications Analysis

826. The problem with Reward & Recognition Programs is that the truly deserving people all too often get left out. How can you make it practical?

827. Does every department have to have a Telecommunications Analysis project Manager on staff?

828. Do you have an Enterprise Telecommunications Analysis project Management Office (EPMO)?

829. Are the products of your organizations Telecommunications Analysis projects meeting customers objectives?

830. What is to be done?

831. Will the staff do training or is that done by a third party?

832. Are your organizations Telecommunications Analysis projects more successful over time?

833. How does this product, good, or service meet the needs of the Telecommunications Analysis project and your organization as a whole?

834. Is there evidence that staff is taking a more professional approach toward management of your organizations Telecommunications Analysis projects?

835. How it is to be done?

836. When a teams productivity and success depend on collaboration and the efficient flow of information, what generally fails them?

837. How can you make it practical?

838. What specific interest groups do you have in place?

839. Does the product, good, or service already exist within your organization?

840. How will resource planning be done?

841. How much risk is involved?

842. Are the attitudes of staff regarding Telecommunications Analysis project work improving?

843. Does your organization have the means (staff, money, contract, etc.) to produce or to acquire the product, good, or service?

844. Why is it to be done?

# 3.2 Change Request: Telecommunications Analysis

845. Can static requirements change attributes like the size of the change be used to predict reliability in execution?

846. Since there are no change requests in your Telecommunications Analysis project at this point, what must you have before you begin?

847. How can you ensure that changes have been made properly?

848. What is the relationship between requirements attributes and attributes like complexity and size?

849. Who can suggest changes?

850. Which requirements attributes affect the risk to reliability the most?

851. What has an inspector to inspect and to check?

852. Will the change use memory to the extent that other functions will be not have sufficient memory to operate effectively?

853. Can you answer what happened, who did it, when did it happen, and what else will be affected?

854. Will there be a change request form in use?

855. Are there requirements attributes that are strongly related to the occurrence of defects and failures?

856. How well do experienced software developers predict software change?

857. Who is responsible to authorize changes?

858. Will all change requests be unconditionally tracked through this process?

859. What is the change request log?

860. How is the change documented (format, content, storage)?

861. Who is communicating the change?

862. What are the requirements for urgent changes?

863. Has your address changed?

# 3.3 Change Log: Telecommunications Analysis

864. How does this relate to the standards developed for specific business processes?

865. Do the described changes impact on the integrity or security of the system?

866. How does this change affect scope?

867. Does the suggested change request represent a desired enhancement to the products functionality?

868. Where do changes come from?

869. Is the submitted change a new change or a modification of a previously approved change?

870. Is the change request open, closed or pending?

871. Is the requested change request a result of changes in other Telecommunications Analysis project(s)?

872. Is this a mandatory replacement?

873. How does this change affect the timeline of the schedule?

874. When was the request submitted?

875. Will the Telecommunications Analysis project fail

if the change request is not executed?

876. Should a more thorough impact analysis be conducted?

877. Who initiated the change request?

878. Is the change backward compatible without limitations?

879. Is the change request within Telecommunications Analysis project scope?

880. When was the request approved?

# 3.4 Decision Log: Telecommunications Analysis

881. Linked to original objective?

882. How do you know when you are achieving it?

883. How effective is maintaining the log at facilitating organizational learning?

884. What is the average size of your matters in an applicable measurement?

885. Does anything need to be adjusted?

886. Who is the decisionmaker?

887. What is the line where eDiscovery ends and document review begins?

888. What makes you different or better than others companies selling the same thing?

889. How does an increasing emphasis on cost containment influence the strategies and tactics used?

890. Is your opponent open to a non-traditional workflow, or will it likely challenge anything you do?

891. Which variables make a critical difference?

892. Behaviors; what are guidelines that the team has

identified that will assist them with getting the most out of team meetings?

893. Who will be given a copy of this document and where will it be kept?

894. What are the cost implications?

895. How does the use a Decision Support System influence the strategies/tactics or costs?

896. What is your overall strategy for quality control / quality assurance procedures?

897. Do strategies and tactics aimed at less than full control reduce the costs of management or simply shift the cost burden?

898. What alternatives/risks were considered?

899. How do you define success?

900. With whom was the decision shared or considered?

# 3.5 Quality Audit: Telecommunications Analysis

901. What are your supplier audits?

902. What are you trying to accomplish with this audit?

903. How does your organization know that its system for commercializing research outputs is appropriately effective and constructive?

904. Can your organization demonstrate exactly how and why results were achieved?

905. How do you indicate the extent to which your personnel would be expected to contribute to the work effort?

906. Are goals well supported with strategies, operational plans, manuals and training?

907. How does your organization know that its financial management system is appropriately effective and constructive?

908. Are there sufficient personnel having the necessary education, background, training, and experience to assure that all operations are correctly performed?

909. How does your organization know that its Strategic Plan is providing the best guidance for the

future of your organization?

910. Are the review comments incorporated?

911. How does your organization know that its system for governing staff behaviour is appropriately effective and constructive?

912. How does your organization know that its security arrangements are appropriately effective and constructive?

913. How does your organization know that its research planning and management systems are appropriately effective and constructive in enabling quality research outcomes?

914. How does your organization know that its promotions system is appropriately effective, constructive and fair?

915. What review processes are in place for your organizations major activities?

916. How does your organization know that its staff financial services are appropriately effective and constructive?

917. Does the supplier use a formal quality system?

918. How does your organization know that the support for its staff is appropriately effective and constructive?

919. How does your organization know that its staffing profile is optimally aligned with the capability

requirements implicit (or explicit) in its Strategic Plan?

920. Will the evidence likely be sufficient and appropriate?

# 3.6 Team Directory: Telecommunications Analysis

921. Decisions: is the most suitable form of contract being used?

922. When will you produce deliverables?

923. Contract requirements complied with?

924. Timing: when do the effects of communication take place?

925. Process decisions: do job conditions warrant additional actions to collect job information and document on-site activity?

926. Process decisions: do invoice amounts match accepted work in place?

927. Process decisions: is work progressing on schedule and per contract requirements?

928. Who will talk to the customer?

929. Who will be the stakeholders on your next Telecommunications Analysis project?

930. Process decisions: are all start-up, turn over and close out requirements of the contract satisfied?

931. How do unidentified risks impact the outcome of the Telecommunications Analysis project?

932. Process decisions: are there any statutory or regulatory issues relevant to the timely execution of work?

933. How will the team handle changes?

934. Have you decided when to celebrate the Telecommunications Analysis projects completion date?

935. Who are the Team Members?

936. Does a Telecommunications Analysis project team directory list all resources assigned to the Telecommunications Analysis project?

937. How does the team resolve conflicts and ensure tasks are completed?

938. Decisions: what could be done better to improve the quality of the constructed product?

939. Process decisions: which organizational elements and which individuals will be assigned management functions?

# 3.7 Team Operating Agreement: Telecommunications Analysis

940. Did you draft the meeting agenda?

941. Do you ensure that all participants know how to use the required technology?

942. What resources can be provided for the team in terms of equipment, space, time for training, protected time and space for meetings, and travel allowances?

943. What are some potential sources of conflict among team members?

944. Do you solicit member feedback about meetings and what would make them better?

945. What administrative supports will be put in place to support the team and the teams supervisor?

946. Are team roles clearly defined and accepted?

947. Resource allocation: how will individual team members account for time and expenses, and how will this be allocated in the team budget?

948. Did you delegate tasks such as taking meeting minutes, presenting a topic and soliciting input?

949. Why does your organization want to participate in teaming?

950. What is your unique contribution to your organization?

951. Reimbursements: how will the team members be reimbursed for expenses and time commitments?

952. What are the current caseload numbers in the unit?

953. Have you set the goals and objectives of the team?

954. Are there more than two functional areas represented by your team?

955. Must your members collaborate successfully to complete Telecommunications Analysis projects?

956. Did you determine the technology methods that best match the messages to be communicated?

957. What is the anticipated procedure (recruitment, solicitation of volunteers, or assignment) for selecting team members?

958. How does teaming fit in with overall organizational goals and meet organizational needs?

959. What is teaming?

# 3.8 Team Performance Assessment: Telecommunications Analysis

960. How do you encourage members to learn from each other?

961. Effects of crew composition on crew performance: Does the whole equal the sum of its parts?

962. To what degree can the team ensure that all members are individually and jointly accountable for the teams purpose, goals, approach, and work-products?

963. Can familiarity breed backup?

964. How does Telecommunications Analysis project termination impact Telecommunications Analysis project team members?

965. To what degree do team members frequently explore the teams purpose and its implications?

966. To what degree will new and supplemental skills be introduced as the need is recognized?

967. To what degree are the goals realistic?

968. To what degree are fresh input and perspectives systematically caught and added (for example, through information and analysis, new members, and senior sponsors)?

969. Delaying market entry: how long is too long?

970. To what degree does the teams approach to its work allow for modification and improvement over time?

971. Lack of method variance in self-reported affect and perceptions at work: Reality or artifact?

972. To what degree do team members understand one anothers roles and skills?

973. To what degree will the approach capitalize on and enhance the skills of all team members in a manner that takes into consideration other demands on members of the team?

974. To what degree can team members meet frequently enough to accomplish the teams ends?

975. Do you give group members authority to make at least some important decisions?

976. To what degree are the skill areas critical to team performance present?

977. To what degree will the team adopt a concrete, clearly understood, and agreed-upon approach that will result in achievement of the teams goals?

978. Social categorization and intergroup behaviour: Does minimal intergroup discrimination make social identity more positive?

979. How do you keep key people outside the group

informed about its accomplishments?

# 3.9 Team Member Performance Assessment: Telecommunications Analysis

980. How should adaptive assessments be implemented?

981. Did training work?

982. To what extent did the evaluation influence the instructional path, such as with adaptive testing?

983. What types of learning are targeted (e.g., cognitive, affective, psychomotor, procedural)?

984. Goals met?

985. What is the role of the Reviewer?

986. What is the target group for instruction (e.g., individual and collective or small team instruction)?

987. What is needed for effective data teams?

988. Does the rater (supervisor) have the authority or responsibility to tell an employee that the employees performance is unsatisfactory?

989. How do you create a self-sustaining capacity for a collaborative culture?

990. How will you identify your Team Leaders?

991. To what degree is there a sense that only the team can succeed?

992. Does statute or regulation require the job responsibility?

993. To what degree are the goals ambitious?

994. What evidence supports your decision-making?

995. How do you make use of research?

996. What are they responsible for?

997. Are any validation activities performed?

# 3.10 Issue Log: Telecommunications Analysis

998. Is the issue log kept in a safe place?

999. What are the typical contents?

1000. Why multiple evaluators?

1001. Which stakeholders can influence others?

1002. What is the stakeholders political influence?

1003. Who is the stakeholder?

1004. What help do you and your team need from the stakeholders?

1005. How often do you engage with stakeholders?

1006. Can an impact cause deviation beyond team, stage or Telecommunications Analysis project tolerances?

1007. What would have to change?

1008. Are the Telecommunications Analysis project issues uniquely identified, including to which product they refer?

1009. What is a change?

1010. How do you reply to this question; you am new

here and managing this major program. How do you suggest you build your network?

1011. Why do you manage human resources?

1012. Who is involved as you identify stakeholders?

1013. Why do you manage communications?

1014. What is the status of the issue?

# 4.0 Monitoring and Controlling Process Group: Telecommunications Analysis

1015. Were escalated issues resolved promptly?

1016. What are the goals of the program?

1017. What communication items need improvement?

1018. Are the services being delivered?

1019. How well did the team follow the chosen processes?

1020. What is the timeline?

1021. When will the Telecommunications Analysis project be done?

1022. Is there adequate validation on required fields?

1023. How is agile portfolio management done?

1024. User: who wants the information and what are they interested in?

1025. How well did you do?

1026. Is there sufficient time allotted between the general system design and the detailed system design phases?

1027. What resources are necessary?

1028. How well did the chosen processes fit the needs of the Telecommunications Analysis project?

1029. What departments are involved in its daily operation?

1030. How do you monitor progress?

1031. Is there sufficient funding available for this?

1032. Is the program in place as intended?

# 4.1 Project Performance Report: Telecommunications Analysis

1033. To what degree will each member have the opportunity to advance his or her professional skills in all three of the above categories while contributing to the accomplishment of the teams purpose and goals?

1034. To what degree can the cognitive capacity of individuals accommodate the flow of information?

1035. To what degree is there centralized control of information sharing?

1036. What is the degree to which rules govern information exchange between individuals within your organization?

1037. To what degree does the information network provide individuals with the information they require?

1038. To what degree are the demands of the task compatible with and converge with the mission and functions of the formal organization?

1039. What degree are the relative importance and priority of the goals clear to all team members?

1040. What is the PRS?

1041. How can Telecommunications Analysis project sustainability be maintained?

1042. To what degree does the team possess adequate membership to achieve its ends?

1043. To what degree do team members agree with the goals, relative importance, and the ways in which achievement will be measured?

1044. To what degree will the team ensure that all members equitably share the work essential to the success of the team?

1045. How will procurement be coordinated with other Telecommunications Analysis project aspects, such as scheduling and performance reporting?

1046. To what degree are the members clear on what they are individually responsible for and what they are jointly responsible for?

1047. To what degree can all members engage in open and interactive considerations?

1048. To what degree does the teams work approach provide opportunity for members to engage in fact-based problem solving?

# 4.2 Variance Analysis: Telecommunications Analysis

1049. At what point should variances be isolated and brought to the attention of the management?

1050. What are the actual costs to date?

1051. Are all authorized tasks assigned to identified organizational elements?

1052. Are data elements reconcilable between internal summary reports and reports forwarded to the stakeholders?

1053. Can the contractor substantiate work package and planning package budgets?

1054. How do you identify and isolate causes of favorable and unfavorable cost and schedule variances?

1055. Are there externalities from having some customers, even if they are unprofitable in the short run?

1056. Is budgeted cost for work performed calculated in a manner consistent with the way work is planned?

1057. How do you verify authorization to proceed with all authorized work?

1058. Is data disseminated to the contractors

management timely, accurate, and usable?

1059. Are authorized changes being incorporated in a timely manner?

1060. Does the accounting system provide a basis for auditing records of direct costs chargeable to the contract?

1061. How do you manage changes in the nature of the overhead requirements?

1062. Other relevant issues of Variance Analysis -selling price or gross margin?

1063. What business event causes fluctuations?

1064. What are the direct labor dollars and/or hours?

1065. How are material, labor, and overhead variances calculated and recorded?

# 4.3 Earned Value Status: Telecommunications Analysis

1066. When is it going to finish?

1067. How does this compare with other Telecommunications Analysis projects?

1068. If earned value management (EVM) is so good in determining the true status of a Telecommunications Analysis project and Telecommunications Analysis project its completion, why is it that hardly any one uses it in information systems related Telecommunications Analysis projects?

1069. Earned value can be used in almost any Telecommunications Analysis project situation and in almost any Telecommunications Analysis project environment. it may be used on large Telecommunications Analysis projects, medium sized Telecommunications Analysis projects, tiny Telecommunications Analysis projects (in cut-down form), complex and simple Telecommunications Analysis projects and in any market sector. some people, of course, know all about earned value, they have used it for years - but perhaps not as effectively as they could have?

1070. Are you hitting your Telecommunications Analysis projects targets?

1071. What is the unit of forecast value?

1072. Where is evidence-based earned value in your organization reported?

1073. Validation is a process of ensuring that the developed system will actually achieve the stakeholders desired outcomes; Are you building the right product? What do you validate?

1074. Where are your problem areas?

1075. How much is it going to cost by the finish?

1076. Verification is a process of ensuring that the developed system satisfies the stakeholders agreements and specifications; Are you building the product right? What do you verify?

# 4.4 Risk Audit: Telecommunications Analysis

1077. Is the customer willing to establish rapid communication links with the developer?

1078. Have top software and customer managers formally committed to support the Telecommunications Analysis project?

1079. Are procedures developed to respond to foreseeable emergencies and communicated to all involved?

1080. Do you have a mechanism for managing change?

1081. Will an appropriate standard of care be applied to all involved?

1082. Are the software tools integrated with each other?

1083. What does internal control mean in the context of the audit process?

1084. What are the risks that could stop you from achieving your objectives?

1085. Are staff committed for the duration of the product?

1086. Is all required equipment available?

1087. Are risk assessments documented?

1088. Are policies communicated to all affected?

1089. Does your auditor understand your business?

1090. Is the technology to be built new to your organization?

1091. Can analytical tests provide evidence that is as strong as evidence from traditional substantive tests?

1092. Do you have position descriptions for all office bearers/staff?

1093. What responsibilities for quality, errors, and outcomes have been delegated to staff (or others) without adequate oversight?

1094. Have reasonable steps been taken to reduce the risks to acceptable levels?

1095. For paid staff, does your organization comply with the minimum conditions for employment and/or the applicable modern award?

1096. What is the Board doing to assure measurement and improve outcomes and quality and reduce avoidable adverse events?

# 4.5 Contractor Status Report: Telecommunications Analysis

1097. What was the final actual cost?

1098. What was the budget or estimated cost for your organizations services?

1099. If applicable; describe your standard schedule for new software version releases. Are new software version releases included in the standard maintenance plan?

1100. How long have you been using the services?

1101. What was the actual budget or estimated cost for your organizations services?

1102. How is risk transferred?

1103. Who can list a Telecommunications Analysis project as organization experience, your organization or a previous employee of your organization?

1104. Describe how often regular updates are made to the proposed solution. Are corresponding regular updates included in the standard maintenance plan?

1105. What process manages the contracts?

1106. What is the average response time for answering a support call?

1107. Are there contractual transfer concerns?

1108. What was the overall budget or estimated cost?

1109. What are the minimum and optimal bandwidth requirements for the proposed solution?

# 4.6 Formal Acceptance: Telecommunications Analysis

1110. Do you perform formal acceptance or burn-in tests?

1111. How well did the team follow the methodology?

1112. Did the Telecommunications Analysis project manager and team act in a professional and ethical manner?

1113. Was the Telecommunications Analysis project managed well?

1114. General estimate of the costs and times to complete the Telecommunications Analysis project?

1115. Have all comments been addressed?

1116. What features, practices, and processes proved to be strengths or weaknesses?

1117. Was the sponsor/customer satisfied?

1118. What are the requirements against which to test, Who will execute?

1119. Do you buy-in installation services?

1120. Who supplies data?

1121. Does it do what client said it would?

1122. What lessons were learned about your Telecommunications Analysis project management methodology?

1123. Was the Telecommunications Analysis project goal achieved?

1124. What can you do better next time?

1125. Was the Telecommunications Analysis project work done on time, within budget, and according to specification?

1126. Do you buy pre-configured systems or build your own configuration?

1127. Did the Telecommunications Analysis project achieve its MOV?

1128. How does your team plan to obtain formal acceptance on your Telecommunications Analysis project?

1129. Is formal acceptance of the Telecommunications Analysis project product documented and distributed?

# 5.0 Closing Process Group: Telecommunications Analysis

1130. What were the actual outcomes?

1131. What do you need to do?

1132. What could have been improved?

1133. Did you do what you said you were going to do?

1134. Did the Telecommunications Analysis project management methodology work?

1135. How will staff learn how to use the deliverables?

1136. Did the Telecommunications Analysis project team have enough people to execute the Telecommunications Analysis project plan?

1137. What is the Telecommunications Analysis project name and date of completion?

1138. Were the outcomes different from the already stated planned?

1139. Was the schedule met?

1140. Will the Telecommunications Analysis project deliverable(s) replace a current asset or group of assets?

1141. Who are the Telecommunications Analysis

project stakeholders?

1142. What is the amount of funding and what Telecommunications Analysis project phases are funded?

1143. How will you do it?

1144. Are there funding or time constraints?

1145. Does the close educate others to improve performance?

# 5.1 Procurement Audit: Telecommunications Analysis

1146. Does the department have a procurement strategy and is it implemented?

1147. Is an appropriated degree of standardization of goods and services respected?

1148. Do the buyers always select or authorize the source of supply on other than contract purchases?

1149. Do procedures require cash advances to be returned by transferred or terminated employees before they can receive final paychecks?

1150. Are information technology resources (e-procurement) used to reduce costs?

1151. How do you ensure whether the goods were supplied or works executed in time and properly recorded in measurement books and stock/works registers after inspection?

1152. Did your organization decide for an appropriate and admissible procurement procedure?

1153. Was suitability of candidates accurately assessed?

1154. Are the right skills, experiences and competencies present in the acquisition workgroup and are the necessary outside specialists involved in part of the process?

1155. Are outsourcing and Public Private Partnerships considered as alternatives to in-house work?

1156. Has an upper limit of cost been fixed?

1157. Does the department evaluate and benchmark the performance of the procurement function/ unit against other comparable procurement functions/ units?

1158. Which are main risks and controls of each phase?

1159. Was the tender clearly and properly specified, including evaluation criteria and knowing about the market and therefore not over-prescriptive and receptive to innovation?

1160. Was the estimated contract value in line with the final cost of the contract awarded?

1161. Do the employees have the necessary skills and experience to carry out procurements efficiently?

1162. Is your organization transparent about winning bids and prices?

1163. Does your organization have an overall strategy and/or policy on public procurement, providing guidance for procuring entities?

1164. When performance conditions were detailed in the tender documentation, did the contracting authority verify if the tenders received met the already stated requirements?

1165. Was the submission of variant tenders accepted and duly ruled?

# 5.2 Contract Close-Out: Telecommunications Analysis

1166. Have all contracts been closed?

1167. Parties: who is involved?

1168. Change in knowledge?

1169. Was the contract sufficiently clear so as not to result in numerous disputes and misunderstandings?

1170. Has each contract been audited to verify acceptance and delivery?

1171. Why Outsource?

1172. Are the signers the authorized officials?

1173. Have all acceptance criteria been met prior to final payment to contractors?

1174. Change in circumstances?

1175. How/when used ?

1176. Parties: Authorized?

1177. Have all contracts been completed?

1178. Was the contract type appropriate?

1179. What is capture management?

1180. Change in attitude or behavior?

1181. Was the contract complete without requiring numerous changes and revisions?

1182. How is the contracting office notified of the automatic contract close-out?

1183. What happens to the recipient of services?

1184. How does it work?

1185. Have all contract records been included in the Telecommunications Analysis project archives?

# 5.3 Project or Phase Close-Out: Telecommunications Analysis

1186. Did the Telecommunications Analysis project management methodology work?

1187. What went well?

1188. What stakeholder group needs, expectations, and interests are being met by the Telecommunications Analysis project?

1189. What information did each stakeholder need to contribute to the Telecommunications Analysis projects success?

1190. Planned completion date?

1191. What benefits or impacts does the stakeholder group expect to obtain as a result of the Telecommunications Analysis project?

1192. Who controlled key decisions that were made?

1193. Is there a clear cause and effect between the activity and the lesson learned?

1194. Does the lesson describe a function that would be done differently the next time?

1195. What security considerations needed to be addressed during the procurement life cycle?

1196. In preparing the Lessons Learned report, should it reflect a consensus viewpoint, or should the report reflect the different individual viewpoints?

1197. What is the information level of detail required for each stakeholder?

1198. How much influence did the stakeholder have over others?

1199. What was learned?

1200. What can you do better next time, and what specific actions can you take to improve?

1201. Have business partners been involved extensively, and what data was required for them?

1202. What was expected from each stakeholder?

1203. What are they?

# 5.4 Lessons Learned: Telecommunications Analysis

1204. How comprehensive was integration testing?

1205. How clearly defined were the objectives for this Telecommunications Analysis project?

1206. How much flexibility is there in the funding (e.g., what authorities does the program manager have to change to the specifics of the funding within the overall funding ceiling)?

1207. What is the frequency of communication?

1208. What is in the future?

1209. What worked well?

1210. What is the expected lifespan of the deliverable?

1211. What is the impact of tax policy on the case?

1212. Would you spend your own time fixing this issue?

1213. How useful was your testing?

1214. Who has execution authority?

1215. How useful was the content of the training you received in preparation for the use of the product/ service?

1216. What is the quality and content of communication?

1217. How useful and complete was the Telecommunications Analysis project document repository?

1218. Were any objectives unmet?

1219. How effective was the support you received during implementation of the product/service?

1220. How mature are the observations?

1221. How satisfied are you with your involvement in the development and/or review of the Telecommunications Analysis project Scope during Telecommunications Analysis project Initiation and Planning?

1222. How effectively were issues resolved before escalation was necessary?

1223. What are the expectations of the individuals?

# Index

already	112, 156-157, 193, 222, 257, 261
altogether	207
always 10, 181, 259
ambitious	240
Amongst	204
amount	25, 258
amounts	232
amplify60, 117
Analysis	1-7, 9-14, 16-31, 33-43, 45-90, 92-138, 140, 142-146, 148, 150-157, 159-161, 163-169, 171, 173-181, 183-187, 189-191, 193-199, 201-209, 211-213, 215-223, 225-227, 229, 232-236, 239, 241, 243-249, 251, 253, 255-259, 262-264, 266-267
analytical	252
analyze	2, 59, 71, 189, 205
analyzed	95
analyzes	141
anothers	237
answer 11-12, 16, 28, 44, 59, 75, 91, 104, 223
answered	27, 42, 58, 74, 90, 103, 128
answering	11, 253
anticipate	150
anyone	39, 105, 126
anything	169, 174, 189, 201, 227
appear	1, 219
appetite	206
applicable	12, 97, 146, 177, 190, 227, 252-253
applied	88, 97, 137, 203, 251
appointed	28, 30
appraise	135
approach	75, 79, 108, 115, 152, 179, 182, 221, 236-237, 246
approaches	82-83, 138, 200
approval	29, 111
approvals	179
approve	144
approved	42, 70, 148, 153, 173, 186, 189, 225-226
approving	148
Architects	8
archived	174, 185
archives	263
around121
articulate	218
artifact237
asking  1, 8, 191

exceed      155, 167
exceeding   56
excellence  8, 38
excellent   53
excessive   202
exchange    245
execute     220, 255, 257
executed    226, 259
Executing   6, 199, 219
execution   92, 187, 223, 233, 266
executive   8, 115, 132
executives  122
Exercise    22, 167
existing 10, 97, 123, 133, 218
expect 264
expected    26, 41, 84, 105-106, 137, 141, 211, 220, 229, 265-266
expend      51
expense     157
expenses    234-235
experience  109-110, 115, 175, 181, 193, 201, 229, 253, 260
experiment  117
expertise   83, 194, 206
experts 40
explained   10
explicit 192, 231
explicitly  108
explore     69, 207, 236
exposure    203
exposures   88
express 135
expressed   130, 140
extent  11, 20, 25, 32, 79, 137-138, 223, 229, 239
external     39, 126, 156
facilitate   11, 17, 101
facilities   206, 213
facing  24, 120
fact-based   246
factors 50, 88, 121, 165, 167, 184, 207, 219
failed   56
failure  47, 118, 121, 174
failures 224
fairly    37

impact 5, 31, 49-51, 53, 56-57, 87, 130, 137, 144, 182, 186, 201, 203, 205, 207, 217, 219, 225-226, 232, 236, 241, 266
impacted        48, 187
impacting       178
impacts         53-54, 138, 201-202, 264
implement       26, 51, 65, 91
implicit 122, 231
importance      245-246
important       20, 22, 40, 61, 70, 108, 119, 122, 125-127, 172, 199, 217, 237
improve         2, 10-11, 64, 75, 77, 79, 81, 83-87, 89-90, 131, 152, 171, 189, 233, 252, 258, 265
improved        76, 81, 90, 100, 135, 257
improving       78, 222
incentives      101
include         23, 83, 144, 211, 214
included        2, 8, 25, 48, 146, 175-176, 184, 253, 263
INCLUDES        10
including       35-36, 38, 48-49, 94, 97, 101, 153, 160, 241, 260
increase        80, 109
increased       107, 195
increasing      119, 227
incurred        45
incurring       157
in-depth        9, 11
indicate        63, 102, 123, 229
indicated       95
indicators      18, 48, 61-62, 70, 76, 94, 206
indirect        53, 156-157, 182
indirectly      1
individual      1, 47, 131, 159, 162, 234, 239, 265
industry        91, 113, 123, 165
infinite 118
influence       79, 120, 131, 134, 137, 199, 227-228, 239, 241, 265
informed        119, 143, 238
ingrained       95
inherent        104
in-house        260
initial    40, 125
initially 32
initiated       150, 184, 226
Initiating      2, 115, 130
Initiation      267

Neutral 11, 16, 28, 44, 59, 75, 91, 104
normal 95
normalized      213
notice 1, 173
notified        199, 213, 218, 263
number          27, 42, 47, 57, 74, 90, 103, 128, 163, 171, 268
numbers         107, 235
numerous        262-263
objection       19
objective       8, 51, 136, 138, 193, 211, 227
objectives      22-23, 26, 28, 32, 36, 62, 97-98, 117-119, 123, 140,
186, 203, 209, 211, 215, 221, 235, 251, 266-267
observe         196
observed        78
observing       187
obsolete        105
obstacles       24, 184
obtain 118, 211, 256, 264
obtained        32, 130, 179
obtaining       52
obviously       11
occurrence      224
occurring       88
occurs 21, 51, 99
offerings       70, 88
office   186-187, 221, 252, 263
officers 213
officials 262
offshore        146
one-time        8
ongoing         86, 92, 161, 176
on-going        180
on-site 232
operate         223
operates        123
operating       6, 47, 100, 157, 234
operation       100, 175, 186, 244
operations      10, 95-96, 101, 186, 229
operators       95, 189
opinions        207
opponent        227
opponents       200
opposed         199

Private 138, 260
problem        16-17, 19-21, 23-25, 28, 32, 38-39, 49, 62, 71, 221,
246, 250
problems       16, 18, 22, 24, 76, 82, 88, 95, 136-137, 146, 202
procedural     239
procedure      235, 259
procedures     10, 93-94, 100, 169, 179, 185, 189, 191, 215-216,
228, 251, 259
proceed        247
process        1-4, 6-8, 10, 28, 30-31, 34, 38, 40, 42, 60-61, 64,
66-67, 69-74, 78, 83, 91-93, 95-96, 98, 100-102, 130-131, 137, 139-
140, 145-148, 151-153, 159-160, 169, 174, 176, 180, 185, 187, 191,
197, 202, 205, 207, 211, 213, 218-220, 224, 232-233, 243, 250-251,
253, 257, 260
processes      50-51, 59, 62, 64-65, 67-68, 72-73, 97, 101, 138,
152-153, 187, 191, 207, 220, 225, 230, 243-244, 255
procuring      260
produce        63, 138, 170, 220, 222, 232
produced       68, 83
produces       163
producing      148, 151
product        1, 48, 61, 70, 105, 108, 153, 165-166, 185-186, 202,
207, 220-222, 233, 241, 250-251, 256, 266-267
production     40, 86, 107, 135
products       1, 17-18, 53, 123-124, 133, 138, 148, 219, 221, 225
profile 230
profit   190
program        21, 53, 64, 94, 137, 195, 201, 204, 219, 242-244,
266
programme      220
Programs       138, 221
progress       29, 46, 89, 97, 116, 126, 138, 179, 183, 192, 216,
219, 244
project 2-4, 6-9, 21, 24-26, 34, 50, 59, 61, 66, 92, 98, 100, 105, 114,
118-120, 122, 124, 129-140, 142-146, 148, 150-156, 159-161, 164-
168, 171, 173-181, 183-186, 194, 196-199, 201-208, 211-213, 215-
223, 225-226, 232-233, 236, 241, 243-246, 249, 251, 253, 255-258,
263-264, 266-267
projected      156-157, 193-194
projects       2, 45, 129, 132, 148, 151, 154, 174, 177, 181, 197-
198, 203, 205-206, 212, 219, 221, 233, 235, 249, 264
promising      108
promote        53, 63, 214

requiring    134, 263
research    17, 108, 117, 165, 229-230, 240
reserved    1
reside  76, 211-212
resistance    217
resolution    62, 82
resolve 17-18, 24, 233
resolved    178, 189, 243, 267
Resource    4-5, 144, 160, 163, 169, 171, 197, 201, 222, 234
resources    2, 8, 17, 22-23, 30, 39, 61, 91, 96, 101, 104, 118,
127, 135, 138, 144, 150, 152, 156, 162-164, 167, 171, 174, 180,
183, 193, 206, 211, 217, 233-234, 242, 244, 259
respect    1
respected    259
respective    137
respond    251
responded    12
response    17, 21, 93, 95-96, 98, 102, 253
responses    115
responsive    175, 183
restrict 146
result    67, 83, 86, 184, 190, 225, 237, 262, 264
resulted    97
resulting    65, 151
results  9, 40-41, 70, 75, 78, 80, 83-84, 87-89, 94, 102, 130, 137-
138, 141, 174, 181-183, 187, 193, 219-220, 229
retain  104, 188
retained    65
retention    48
return 83, 113, 191, 207
returned    259
returns 190
revenue    21, 49
revenues    54
review 10, 40, 70, 132, 168, 188, 193, 211, 227, 230, 267
reviewed    30, 131
Reviewer    239
reviews 168, 193, 201
revised 63, 97, 156
revisions    263
reward 47, 53, 67, 221
rewarded    24
rewards    101

rework  45, 53
rights    1
robustness      135
rolling   159
routine 99
safety   123
sampling        179, 188
satisfied        182, 232, 255, 267
satisfies 250
satisfy   130
satisfying       107
savings 42, 44, 48, 63
scalable        79
scenario        35, 42, 220
schedule        3-4, 38, 93, 122, 157, 159-160, 168, 177-178, 186,
193, 197, 201, 203, 211, 215, 219, 225, 232, 247, 253, 257
scheduled       181
schedules       157, 167
scheduling      160, 194, 198, 246
scheme 98
Science  61, 176
scientific       176
Scorecard       2, 12-14
scorecards      101
Scores  14
scoring 10
screening       140, 189
seamless        108
second  12
section 12, 27, 42, 57-58, 74, 90, 103, 128
sector   249
securing        56, 121
security        23, 69, 85, 92, 100, 134, 152, 187, 225, 230, 264
segment 218
segments        37, 107
select  96, 259
selected        85, 87, 140, 143, 183
selecting       68, 110, 140, 220, 235
Selection       5, 213
seller   182, 211
sellers  1
selling  117, 166, 227
-selling 248

strengths       152, 165, 255
stretch 116
strict    73
strive    116, 174
strong  252
Strongly        11, 16, 28, 44, 59, 75, 91, 104, 224
structure       3-4, 114, 123, 151, 154, 171, 206, 217
structured      116, 179
stubborn        126
stupid  106
subdivided      193
subject9-10, 40
subjective      145
subjects        68
submission      261
submitted       225
subset 21
succeed 52, 123, 165, 240
success         18-19, 31, 34, 40-41, 44, 47, 52, 55, 77, 82-83, 87,
97, 108, 110, 112-113, 116, 118, 121, 123, 131, 152, 167, 174, 218,
222, 228, 246, 264
successes       108
successful      60, 83, 85, 100, 120, 125, 132, 137, 171, 221
succession      93
successor       159
suddenly        205
sufficient      206, 223, 229, 231, 243-244
suggest         206, 223, 242
suggested       95, 185, 225
suitable        205, 232
summary         247
supervisor      234, 239
supplied        259
supplier        106, 229-230
suppliers       31, 69-70, 113
supplies        255
supply 53, 135, 259
support         8, 22, 60, 89, 99-100, 102, 119, 122, 132-133, 143,
169, 208, 218, 228, 230, 234, 251, 253, 267
supported       68, 205, 219, 229
supporters      135
supporting      80, 96, 179, 192
supports        234, 240